SORCHA MAHONY
LARISSA POPLE

LIFE IN THE DEBT TRAP

Stories of children and families struggling
with debt

POLICY PRESS **SHORTS** INSIGHTS

First published in Great Britain in 2018 by

Policy Press
University of Bristol
1-9 Old Park Hill
Bristol
BS2 8BB
UK
t: +44 (0)117 954 5940
pp-info@bristol.ac.uk
www.policypress.co.uk

North America office:
Policy Press
c/o The University of Chicago Press
1427 East 60th Street
Chicago, IL 60637, USA
t: +1 773 702 7700
f: +1 773 702 9756
sales@press.uchicago.edu
www.press.uchicago.edu

British Library Cataloguing in Publication Data
A catalogue record for this book is available from the British Library.

Library of Congress Cataloging-in-Publication Data
A catalog record for this book has been requested.

ISBN 978-1-4473-4109-3 (paperback)
ISBN 978-1-4473-4110-9 (ePub)
ISBN 978-1-4473-4111-6 (Mobi)
ISBN 978-1-4473-4112-3 (ePDF)

The right of Sorcha Mahony and Larissa Pople to be identified as authors of this work has been asserted by them in accordance with the Copyright, Designs and Patents Act 1988.

The statements and opinions contained within this publication are solely those of the authors and not of the University of Bristol or Policy Press. The University of Bristol and Policy Press disclaim responsibility for any injury to persons or property resulting from any material published in this publication.

Policy Press works to counter discrimination on grounds of gender, race, disability, age and sexuality.

Cover design by Policy Press
Front cover: image kindly supplied by Alamy
Printed and bound in Great Britain by CMP, Poole
Policy Press uses environmentally responsible print partners

We would like to dedicate this book to our participants, as a way of thanking them for the contributions they have made to the research, and through this to the wider campaign for giving respite to families struggling with problem debt.

"It got to a point where I was really, really struggling and I was basically trying to buy time with people that I owed money to and, you know, people like gas, electric. And I can't remember who I spoke to, but I had phoned someone the previous week. I don't know whether it was a phone company or whatever. I explained that I couldn't pay my bill and explained, you know, said I was prepared to make a payment but I couldn't pay the bill in full. And the person on the end of the phone was so judgemental. And I had made a comment about, you know, 'Look, I'm trying to be honest with you and upfront with you in saying that there is this circumstance, there's this circumstance and it's hard but I'm doing my best.' And he said something along the lines of: 'Oh, don't give me that excuse.' And I was so shocked at his response that I just didn't know what to say ... I was trying to manage my own sort of like finances and speak to people on the other end of the phone, but they were so judgemental. It was as if they were making the assumption that I was a certain type of person. And I said to this lad on the phone who had made that comment, I said: 'How dare you speak to me like that.' ... I said: 'I am struggling and I'm struggling hard.' I said: 'I don't have holidays. I don't buy expensive clothes. I don't go on an expensive night out. I'm just basically trying to make ends meet.' I said: 'How dare you judge me.'" (Pam, working mother of three, who fell into problem debt following her divorce)

'All these moral dramas [surrounding debt] start from the assumption that personal debt is ultimately a matter of self-indulgence, a sin against one's loved ones – and therefore, that redemption must necessarily be a matter of purging and restoration of ascetic self-denial. What's being shunted out of sight here is first of all the fact that everyone is now in debt … and that very little of this debt was accrued by those determined to find money to bet on the horses or toss away on fripperies … it was mainly to be given to children, to share with friends, or otherwise to be able to build and maintain relations with other human beings that are based on something other than sheer material calculation. One must go into debt to achieve a life that goes in any way beyond sheer survival…. For real human beings survival is rarely enough. Nor should it be.' (Graeber, D, 2011, *Debt: The first 5,000 years*, p 379)

Contents

Acknowledgements

This book would not have been possible without input from many, many people. And so, we would like to thank the following:

- All our participants, for allowing us briefly into their lives and for sharing their debt (and other) stories with us.
- Our colleagues at The Children's Society for all their support for the book and their contributions to the research that informs it. In particular we would like to thank: Jim Davis, Angharad Lewis, Helen Maitland, Cath Morris, Jo Petty and Sarah Wayman for conducting some of the interviews on which these stories are based; Annalisa Greene for her input into identifying the key themes in the data; Lucy Capron, Iain Porter and Tom Redfearn for their guidance on the ever-changing policy contexts that shape experiences of debt and wider financial precarity; Sam Royston, Ilona Pinter, Anastasia French and Peter Grigg for their constructive feedback on earlier drafts of the typescript; and Lily Holman-Brant for lending her communications expertise to the project. And again our thanks go to Sam Royston for his input into the discussion around policy recommendations.
- Dorothea Mueller for her contribution to the fieldwork and her sharp analytical insights.
- Emily Smeaton from Paradigm Research for contributing to the fieldwork.
- StepChange Debt Charity for their partnership working on the initial research project, and especially Joe Sturtees for his later guidance on the policy contexts.

- Sam Thompson for his advice on the structure and content of the final chapter.
- The staff at Policy Press for giving us the opportunity to share our participants' stories more widely and for being so supportive during the processes of writing and publishing.

PREFACE

The origins of this book

Sorcha Mahony

In the spring of 2014, The Children's Society employed me on a 12-month contract to provide the maternity cover for one of its senior researchers, Larissa Pople. Before Larissa left for maternity leave, she explained the projects that required oversight in her absence: a qualitative, longitudinal study of poverty in childhood with the University of Bath; and a study of fuel poverty and the effects it can have on children. At the end of our handover meeting, Larissa mentioned that through The Children's Society's Debt Trap research, undertaken in partnership with the debt advice charity StepChange – research that I had been involved in on a freelance basis through conducting interviews with some of the participants – there was a fair amount of qualitative data on children and families' experiences of problem debt, and that we should be thinking about what might be done with the data, beyond the airing that they were already set to receive in the initial report *The debt trap: Exposing the impact of problem debt on children* (The Children's Society and StepChange Debt Charity, 2014).

Over the course of the next year or so, The Children's Society undertook a further three 'spikes' of activity in relation to the Debt

Trap campaign, each of which focused on an element of the original research, explored it in more detail through qualitative and quantitative methods, and saw the publication of a focused report:

- *Playday not payday* (The Children's Society, 2014), which highlighted the problematic use of payday loan advertising to children;
- *Show some warmth* (The Children's Society, 2015a), which exposed the impact of energy debt on families with children;
- *The wolf at the door* (The Children's Society, 2015b), which explored practices of Council Tax debt collection and their effects on families.

Along with colleagues, I conducted some of the qualitative fieldwork for these focused studies, visiting families up and down the country to try to understand their experiences and represent their voices in the reports about the issues they experienced. All the while, Larissa's words rang in my ears, but instead of coming up with ideas about what to do with the qualitative data that we had amassed, we had merely accumulated more until, by the spring of 2015, there were around 55 interview transcripts sitting (securely encrypted) on my hard drive.

In the early summer of 2015, Larissa returned from maternity leave and I stayed on. We discussed the projects that had continued in her absence and I confessed that ideas about what to do with the qualitative debt data had been in short supply, that there had been no lightbulb moment as to what to do with it all.

In parallel to my involvement with the research for the Debt Trap activities, I was becoming increasingly convinced of the power of stories, not only in engaging readers or listeners, but also through that in galvanising support for change. As part of the fuel poverty study, I had reported to the commissioning organisation's board of directors on my findings, and I read out a story I had written that was based on the qualitative data I had collected. When I finished, there was a strange silence in the room, until one of the men in suits shuffled in his seat and made a joke about whether anyone else needed a tissue. I went on to present a PowerPoint slideshow with details of the study's methodology, the overall narrative, the themes and sub-themes I had observed, and the quantitative data that our partners at National Energy Action had collected, but the questions at the end of the presentation were about the story and the fate of the family concerned, and the feedback was on how powerful it had been. Discussion turned to what could be done to support people like those in the story, and I was asked to make a recording of it so that they could share it as a podcast and use it as a lobbying tool.

I was also experiencing the power of stories through discovering two bodies of literature: one of which comprised journalistic and ethnographic accounts of the lived experiences of adversity in developed and developing country contexts; the other of which comprised psychologists' accounts of their clients. These literatures, while disparate, were united in placing human stories at the centre of their narratives and using them to illuminate themes and patterns pertaining to individual experiences, and to shine a light on those aspects of the broader cultural and socioeconomic contexts that gave shape to these. They were underpinned by theoretical frameworks, but these informed rather than dominated the narratives, helping to bring to life ideas that otherwise remain the preserve of an elite few who have the time, resources and inclination to try to penetrate abstract theoretical writing. These literatures were also united in bringing to the fore the relationship between the author/observer and those being studied, adding a further layer of insight into already absorbing topics. I found myself captivated and unable to put the books down, drawn into the lives of the people in them and into new ways of thinking about things I did not even realise I was interested in. When I read Stephen Grosz's (2014) *The examined life*, I had a lightbulb moment. A collection of short stories about his psychoanalysis clients, told with compassion, an expert's insight and a poet's ear, it was a riveting book that gave a strong sense of people's inner worlds and the contexts surrounding them, an insight into Grosz's professional relationships with his clients and an impetus to challenge prevailing norms around mental ill-health.

That was it – that was the answer to the debt data question.

We could attempt something equivalent. We could use our qualitative data to write a collection of short stories about children and families' experiences of problem debt, and we could try to write them in such a way that would engage readers and help to challenge some of the assumptions and pejorative discourses surrounding problem debt. The stories would be accessible and based on participants' narratives, and they would be informed by theory (but not overtly, and not to the distraction of the human side of things). They would refer to relevant aspects of the broader context – policy, cultural, social, academic – and they would offer brief reflections on the process of conducting qualitative research. Okay, so Grosz had based his stories on hours and hours of discussion with each individual he wrote about, whereas we had visited each of our participants for just a couple of hours, but that should not stop us trying – trying to do as much as we could with the stories that people had shared with us.

Our policy and campaigns colleagues had done their bit putting the data to effective use in their reports and lobbying for a statutory Breathing Space scheme – a scheme to prevent families' debts from increasing by freezing interest and charges and pausing enforcement action, allowing families the time and space they need to get back on track. However, there was more to say that lay beyond the scope of that work – more to say about some of the underlying psychosocial themes that had emerged, more to share on the process of conducting the qualitative interviews, more to do in terms of highlighting the ways in which broad structures of inequality play out in the microcosm of people's everyday lives, and more ways to write about the issues, through stories.

I looked through my book collection and scanned the spines for a publisher that might be interested. I called Policy Press, started developing a proposal for a *Shorts* book, and spoke with Larissa:

"I know what to do with the debt data."

"Oh yes? What's that?"

"We write it up into a book of stories."

"*We?*"

"If you want to?"
"Sure."

Around the time that Policy Press commissioned this book, The Children's Society was embarking on a fourth and final spike in the Debt Trap campaign. Through this spike, which explored the relationship between problem debt and children's mental health, Larissa and I – along with other fieldworkers at The Children's Society – visited yet more families struggling with debt, and in some cases revisited families we had met doing the research for the initial *Debt trap* report (The Children's Society and StepChange Debt Charity, 2014). This led to yet more qualitative data, making it 67 transcripts in total, and more substantive and methodological insights that we felt also merited consideration and coverage beyond the exposure they would receive in the publication *The damage of debt* (The Children's Society, 2016a).

At the time of completing the typescript for this book, the Debt Trap campaign was at a climax. It had run for around five years, and involved four spikes and a great deal of behind-the-scenes work on the part of the policy and campaigns staff at The Children's Society along with other debt-related organisations. And it looked as though the hard work was starting to pay off: in late October 2017, the government announced that it would be introducing a statutory Breathing Space scheme and published a consultation on what that might look like in practice, with a view to producing draft legislation in 2019.

The achievement of a statutory Breathing Space scheme was due in no small part to the strength of the evidence base on problem debt, and the way this showcased the effects it can have on people's lives. And at the heart of the evidence base within The Children's Society were the interviews conducted with children and families. This book is the result of re-analysing those interviews, reflecting on the process of undertaking them and considering some of the underlying themes and wider contexts they point to. It marks an attempt to look beyond the focus of each of the campaign spikes, to convey some of the less-exposed aspects of people's experiences, to pull in the often-under-acknowledged process of gaining access to these, and to do this using stories as a medium. We offer it as a means of bringing to life our participants' journeys and coping tactics around problem debt, and as a call for more humane policy making towards those who have found themselves living in the debt trap.

Sorcha Mahony

Introduction and methodological note

Sorcha Mahony

Tracy and Simon

From the outside, Tracy's house was much like the other unassuming, terraced houses on the estate: two storeys high, with grey scalloped roof tiles, brown pebble-dash walls and a small front yard strewn with bike tyres, plastic garden furniture and empty plant pots. Tracy had an air about her like that of many other parents living with problem debt: tired, coping and wearing a smile that was almost a sigh. Inside, it smelled of washing powder and cooking oil, and very faintly of cigarette smoke. It was cold, dimly lit and uninviting. Tracy's interview – conducted on her bed in the lino-floored dining room where she slept because her teenage son and daughter occupied both of the bedrooms – revealed a journey into debt that was unique in its detail but familiar in its overall shape: a history of relatively low income, a series of life events that had taken their toll, managed debts in the form of an overdraft, a credit card and a couple of store cards, followed by an income shock (in the form of divorce and reduced income), an inability to service previously managed credit commitments and a spiral into arrears with essential household bills. The interview with Tracy's son, Simon, revealed a story that resonated with some of our other young participants: a knowledge of money problems and an awareness (to a degree) of debt, a sense of missing out on some of the things his peers enjoyed, a palpable feeling of stress in the household, a protective stance towards his mother and a determination to help in whatever ways he could.

Tracy cried when she talked about the stress of living with debt (as opposed to just being poor) and about how hard it was trying to keep it together for the sake of the children. Her eyes lit up when she spoke about her newfound joy of shopping at discount supermarkets, and she got cross when she talked of the loan companies that were *still* sending marketing material through the post. Then, at the end of her interview, she said this:

'I don't like talking about all this, it's been such an awful bit of my life, but I feel like I should. I want to make sure no one else gets into the same situation I did. I want tell people: "Don't get into debt. Get help before it's too late." And I want to ask the government to do more to help them.'

Few other participants articulated so clearly a desire that their contribution be useful in a broader societal sense, and few pointed so lucidly to one of the most fundamental dichotomies in the debate surrounding problem debt: the responsibility that families have in managing their own finances, on the one hand, yet the need for state intervention, on the other – both in preventing people's debts from escalating and in helping to deal with the fallout from those that have become entrenched.

The stories in this book explore this fault line. They reveal the monumental challenges that families like Tracy's can face in the context of their debt journeys, and the far-from-passive responses that people have to the financial predicaments they are in. And they reveal the wider contexts that curb families' capacities to avoid problem debt and to escape from its clutches unscathed once it has taken root.

The bigger picture

Tracy was one of 36 parents who took part in the qualitative research for The Children's Society's Debt Trap campaign between 2013 and

2016, and Simon was one of 17 young people interviewed. Together, when they participated in our research in 2013, they were one of the 1.4 million households with children living with problem debt in the UK, and Simon was one of the 2.4 million young people within these households (The Children's Society and StepChange Debt Charity, 2014, p 104).

Household debt has been increasing in the UK since 2012. Immediately following the 2008 financial crisis, it fell slightly, but has been on the increase again over the past five years, and continues to grow. Two hundred billion pounds of the country's total personal debt burden (which stands at £1.5 trillion and comprises mostly mortgages) is made up of unsecured credit – in the form of credit card debts, overdrafts, hire purchase debts, bank loans, payday loans and store cards (Citizens Advice, 2017). While difficulty repaying these debts may be a short-term issue for some, for others it is more intractable. Either way, the harm that can ensue for individuals and families, for lenders and for the economy as a whole is significant (Citizens Advice, 2017).

According to analysis by Citizens Advice of the UK's Wealth and Assets survey data, couples with children and lone parents are much more likely to hold unsecured[1] debts than their counterparts who have no children (Citizens Advice, 2017). According to the organisation's analysis of its own data, those who seek its help for their debt problems are also struggling with other challenges in their lives, including disabilities and long-term health conditions, and problems with their benefits and housing situations (Citizens Advice, 2017). According to StepChange Debt Charity, in its analysis of the data it collected from its clients in the first half of 2017, 18.8% of people who contacted the charity had also faced unemployment or redundancy and 16.6% had experienced injury or illness (StepChange Debt Charity, 2017). In 2017, the charity also reported a reduction in the proportion of people falling into debt because of a lack of budgeting skills (from 20% to 15% between 2016 and 2017), an increase in the average amount of unsecured debt held by those it supports (from £14,251 in 2016 to £14,367 in 2017) and an average of six unsecured debts per client (StepChange Debt Charity, 2017).

This book is about some of the people behind these figures – people like Tracy and Simon whose lives are nested in a broader context that makes it increasingly difficult for families on low incomes to get by without taking on unsecured credit or falling behind with household bills. It is a context defined by government cuts, a 'broken' benefits system and a decrease in purchasing power.

Following the global financial crisis of 2008, the British government embarked on a programme of 'austerity' that is unparalleled in modern history. In the name of repaying the country's national debt, the Conservative-led coalition government, followed by the Conservative government, cut budgets across central and local government to the tune of tens of billions of pounds, which resulted in the closure of fundamental local services across the country – often the cornerstone of community life for people on low incomes.

Meanwhile, the welfare system has been undergoing the biggest reform since its inception in the post-war years, with many key benefits being first delinked from the Retail Price Index in 2010 (and thereby increasing below the rate of inflation), then capped in 2012 and frozen in 2015, and with others taking major cash cuts while sanctions were applied with increasing alacrity (Royston, 2017).

In addition, between 2008 and 2014, average weekly earnings in the UK fell in real terms (that is, consumer prices, for things such as housing and food, rose faster than wages, meaning that people's purchasing power decreased), and since 2014 real wage growth in the UK has been either low or stagnant (O'Leary, 2017). By October 2017, the inflation rate stood at a five-year high of around 3% – almost 1% above the rate of wage growth (BBC News, 2017).

What all of this means for people like Tracy and Simon, for the other families in our debt research and for the 1.4 million families also dealing with problem debt in the UK, is that the context in which they are living makes it increasingly hard to manage financially without borrowing money.

Debt, problem debt and poverty

In this book we use the term 'debt' to refer to unsecured personal or household borrowing. This might take the form of bank loans, payday loans, overdrafts, credit cards, store cards, hire-purchase schemes, catalogue accounts or doorstep loans. We also use the term to refer to arrears on household bills such as those for Council Tax, gas, electricity, water, the television, the telephone and broadband packages. We use the term 'problem debt' to refer to situations where families are not able to keep up with repayments on what they have borrowed or what they owe to creditors for services provided, although the precise definitions have varied in line with the different elements of the Debt Trap campaign – discussed more fully below.

While the book and the research behind it is about problem debt, poverty was a feature in most of the households where we conducted the qualitative interviews. Indeed, The Children's Society's interest within the Debt Trap campaign has been in families experiencing the combination of problem debt and a low income. We took a broad and flexible approach to conceptualising poverty and operationalising it in the context of sampling and recruitment. In some cases, it was established through entitlement to free school meals – a common proxy indicator for child poverty, albeit one with recognised limitations (see for example Hobbs and Vignoles, 2007). In other cases, poverty was established through household incomes being below 60% of the median equivalised household income in the UK; and in still other cases, while incomes may have been higher than 60% of the median household income in the UK (though not by much), they did not stretch far enough to cover household expenditure after debt repayments were taken into account. In only a couple of cases would participant households be considered not to have low incomes, although even here – as above – once servicing debts was considered, remaining incomes were not sufficient to pay for the upkeep of the family. What this means in terms of our sample is that in most participant households, problem debt and poverty co-exist, and in many cases debts have become problematic *because of* low incomes and shocks to fragile household budgets.[2] Also in many cases – especially in interviews with children and young people – poverty and problem debt seem to be inextricably woven together in the way they are experienced, and this is reflected in participants' narratives and the stories that draw from them.

Methodological note

Data collection and sampling

The data on which the stories in this book are based were collected as part of the Debt Trap campaign at The Children's Society. This began in 2013 and entailed five rounds of intensive campaigning activity, four of which were supported by qualitative interviews with parents and young people living in households struggling with debt. The first set of interviews, conducted in 2013, explored people's journeys into debt and the effects on household members in very broad terms. There were 15 parents and six young people in this initial sample. Through this round of activity, an additional three areas of interest were identified – over time – as warranting focused campaigning activity and further in-depth interviews:

- experiences of Council Tax debt;
- experiences of energy debt;
- experiences of mental health difficulties in the context of debt problems.

The focus on Council Tax debt entailed in-depth interviews with a further six parents and three young people, as well as two care leavers, conducted in 2014. The focus on energy debt entailed interviews with an additional eight parents and eight young people, also conducted in 2014. And the focus on debt and mental health difficulties entailed interviews with 13 parents and six young people, some of whom were in the original sample for the initial Debt Trap campaign spike, and were conducted in 2016. This brought the total number of participants to 55 (36 parents, 17 children and two care leavers) and the total number of interview transcripts to 67. In all cases except those of care leavers, the young people interviewed were children of parent interviewees.

Adult participants were invited to take part in interviews through various channels: through StepChange Debt Charity, through The Children's Society's practice base and through a research recruitment agency. Sampling criteria varied according to the element of the Debt Trap Campaign:

- for the initial research, participants had to be in arrears on at least one credit commitment or household bill;
- for the research into Council Tax debt, participants had to be behind with Council Tax payments by two or more months, had to have forfeited the option to pay by instalments or had to still owe money from the previous year's Council Tax bill;
- for the research into energy debt, participants had to have received an energy bill three months previously but not yet paid it in full, missed a direct debit payment or had a debt on their pre-payment account over £100;
- for the research into debt and mental health difficulties we took a more open approach to sampling: participants had to have had experience of living with low income and debt at some point, with the interpretation of what this looked like in practice defined subjectively by interviewees, as well as experience of struggling psychologically in the context of these.

Young people were recruited through two channels: mainly through parents who had agreed to be interviewed and were comfortable inviting their children to take part, and – in the case of care leavers – through services that supported them. All participants were given high-street gift vouchers after their interviews, as a token of thanks for their contributions.

The interviews with parents involved a timeline approach, whereby they were shown a timeline (flexible in terms of actual dates) and asked to talk about key points on their debt journeys (as well as key life events and experiences further back in time and imagined ones going forward), with discussion of the effects of debt and their coping tactics built around this. We took the same approach in the more focused interviews (on Council Tax debt, energy debt, and debt and mental health difficulties), although discussion in these leaned more heavily towards the particular issue we were interested in. The interviews with young people assumed no knowledge of debt or broader financial struggles. If these were known to young participants, and if they wanted to talk about them, they tended to emerge indirectly through discussion of other interview topics: money and possessions, hobbies and interests, life at home, family and friends, school and neighbourhood and aspirations for the future. If debt and wider money problems were not known to young people, discussions covered the topics above in broad terms.

Key themes, theoretical underpinnings and story construction

Through re-analysis of the interview transcripts, we identified a set of themes – 16 in total – that we felt warranted further attention, either because they had resonance across the sample or because they were particularly striking in some way. Each of these themes is the subject of one of the stories in this book. While, in reality, individual participants' data often covered more than one theme, as a narrative device and for the purpose of clarity we focus on one main theme per story. Each of the stories falls into one of two broader categories: *falling* into problem debt and *responding* (practically and psychologically) to it.

'Falling' and 'responding' stories and themes

Story	Main theme
Falling	
The journey	A typical journey into problem debt.
Isolation	In the context of problem debt, isolation can occur within the household as well as between households.
Loss	Loss can play a central role in the journey into problem debt.
Luxuries and necessities	The distinction between luxuries and necessities is not always clear in the context of problem debt and poverty.
Who cares?	A lack of family support can trigger problem debt and make the smallest of debts problematic.
The elephant in the room/ consumerism	The role of consumerism in people's debt journeys.
Responding	
Guilt	Some parents blame themselves for the predicaments they are in.
The Others	Other parents can engage in the psychological process of 'othering' in the context of problem debt.
Keeping up appearances	Some people feel pressure to keep up appearances – at home as well as outside the home.
The child	Low income and problem debt can make us question the utility and universality of basic conceptual categories such 'child'.
The tyranny of the small things	Small tactics designed to cope with problem debt and low income can, in combination, become overbearing.
Juggling	People commonly juggle problem debts and experience difficulties in doing so.
The downside of help	The journey out of problem debt can entail paying the ultimate price.
The debt premium	Money and time are hidden debt premiums.
Dreams	Living with problem debt can curtail dreams.
The gift	Problem debt can result in an inability to give and there are consequences of this.

Theoretical influences

We identified the themes and stories through (re)immersion in the data, but data do not magically transform themselves into themes and stories. We have interpreted the data, using a set of sociological concepts and inspired by a particular theoretical perspective. Our theoretical foundations are not made explicit in the stories, but they have informed the direction of the narratives, to greater or lesser degrees, and in the interests of transparency it is worth acknowledging them here.

Conceptually we are interested, on the one hand, in *agency* – in people's capacities to act in the world. On the other hand, we are interested in *structures* – in the institutions, norms and values that persist over time and that form the parameters within which agency is exercised. And we are especially interested in what happens at the interface of the two: in the idea that agency, when exercised from a position of socioeconomic disadvantage, can be 'negative' (Jeffrey, 2011) – that is, it can have outcomes that are undesired, undesirable and unintended.

Until quite recently, scholars writing within the so-called 'new social studies of childhood' were mainly concerned with identifying and celebrating the agency that children exercise, on the basis that until the blossoming of this literature, children were not really conceived of as agents in their own right within academia and within educational, political and legal spheres, among others. The idea that children are active agents in their own right is now well established within the childhood studies literature (although there is clearly some way to go for this idea to percolate out into many parts of the wider world), and there is increasing appetite among scholars of childhood and youth – especially within the developing world – to explore some of the complexities that attend it. Inspired by the work of anthropologists and sociologists such as Paul Willis (1977), Phillippe Bourgois (1995) and Pierre Bourdieu (1996), there is an increasing awareness and documentation of the ways in which agency can have unintended outcomes, even alongside desired ones, when exercised from positions of marginalisation (see, for example, Dyson, 2010; Jeffrey, 2011). As already suggested, while we do not explicitly refer to these theoretical influences in the stories that follow, they have informed the way we have interpreted the data and given shape to some of the narratives.

Stories

We use stories as a means of bringing to light the key themes outlined above, and through which to bring to life our theoretical underpinnings. Stories are fundamental to human life. They are one of the key ways in which we make sense of the world around us, of our experiences in it and of our relationship to it. Every day we narrate aspects of our lives to ourselves and others, verbally and through the written word, and we engage with the stories that others tell us. As a nation we consume stories voraciously through newspapers, books, television, film and digital media, and our counterparts the world over do the same, with some leaning more heavily towards the oral tradition. In short, sharing our data in the form of stories is a way of tapping into a universal modus operandi – one that has the potential to hold people's attention in a way that some academic writing and 'grey' literature fails to do. Stories seem to resonate with an inner desire in us all to give shape to the sometimes random-seeming nature of our lives. When we impart information in the form of a story – with a beginning, a middle and an end (of sorts), with key characters and a level of detail that brings readers into the homes and right up close to the people and experiences we are shedding light on – we offer those readers an opportunity to engage with the content through a form that is natural and effortless, and to thereby forge an emotional connection with the subject matter, uninterrupted by jargon.

To preserve anonymity, we constructed each story using data from a number of different participants, we altered certain demographic and biographical details and we gave participants pseudonyms. For each story we selected a family or individual whose experiences and transcript(s) best reflected the main theme, and we then replaced other elements of the story with data from other participants. For the stories whose main focus is on the process of *falling* into problem debt, this meant drawing on other participants for data on responding to problem debt; and for those whose main focus is on *responding*, it meant drawing on other participants for data on falling into problem debt. For all of them it meant using other participants' data on types of debt, on the research setting, on the behaviour in the research encounter and on the methodological and ethical dilemmas we faced conducting the research. We also altered people's locations, family structures and ages.

This means that while the stories are *based on* real data derived from qualitative interviews (and all the quotes are real), the stories themselves are constructs. The ethical risk of identifying people by telling their stories unaltered was too great to write them any other way. There is a precedent for this approach – for example within Byron's (2014) *The skeleton cupboard* – but it does raise important questions, in particular around the potential for over-dramatising events and experiences. In fact, some of our colleagues at The Children's Society expressed this concern when reading early drafts of some of the stories, querying whether we had "lumped all the bad things" from different people's experiences into one (in fact it transpired that the stories that appeared the most unbelievable were actually insufficiently composite and anonymised, in early draft form). Our approach to ensuring that we did not over-dramatise events and experiences was to be conscious of working against the possibility, and to be scrupulous about checking our own stories and each other's, working on the principle that where we drew on other people's data, there was an equivalent experience and the story overall was feasible according to our joint knowledge of the dataset as a whole – that is, that there were real stories within the dataset that were similar, but they were sufficiently different to make it impossible to identify actual participants.

Once we had crafted the initial stories, we went back through each one and added discussion on a relevant policy context, and brief reference to some aspect of the process of conducting the research. These policy and research process reflections are intended to compliment the stories with relevant contextual information rather than detract from them in any way.

We offer this short collection of stories in the hope that they will shed light on some of the finer-grained detail of people's experiences of falling into and living with problem debt, and inspire a kinder approach to policy making, both in terms of problem debt itself but also in terms of the wider backdrop of socioeconomic inequality that can allow it to take hold.

ONE

The journey

Larissa Pople

Ruth turns up 10 minutes late, a whirlwind of lipstick, bright prints and friendly concern. "Oh my goodness, what time did we say? Come in, come in … Leila, say hello!" Leila hides behind her mother's leg, gazing at the printed material, a fistful of skirt in her tiny hand.

Ruth and her three children – four-year-old Leila, eight-year-old Grace and 15-year-old Matthew – live in a two-up, two-down, purpose-built house in a shabby housing estate in the East Midlands. Ruth started out as a teacher, and it is easy to imagine her in a classroom of 30 unruly teenagers, keeping them in line with her kindly but no-nonsense approach. She resembles one of those favourite aunts who has eyes in the back of her head. There is no point trying to pull the wool over them.

After 10 long years as a teacher, juggling the stress of the classroom with being a single parent, Ruth decided to go back to university to do a PhD, while working concurrently in a charity job to pay the bills. The change in career direction was driven in part by the increasingly uncertain presence of the children's father, who often disappeared from their lives for months on end. Being the main breadwinner, Ruth had to consider whether her job would be compatible with family life, and the university job that she had in mind seemed like a good fit. Then Leila came along unexpectedly, and her hopes of a job in academia were put on hold. For the first two years of Leila's life, Ruth stayed at home to look after her because the income from her old job would not have covered the cost of childcare. But when, in the term after Leila's second birthday, she became eligible for 15 hours of free childcare, Ruth went back to work, earning just over £14,000 a year. Her finances were stretched to their limit, but she was just about able to manage.

In many ways, Ruth's debt story follows a well-worn route similar to many of the other families that we have spoken to. Her credit history was remarkable in its modesty rather than its extravagance, and it was not until she was well into her thirties that she took out her first credit card. With a regular income, she was able to manage her credit commitments well. What is unusual in her story is the trigger for a spiral into problematic debt. In an unfortunate series of events, a miscalculation by her employer about how much she was earning when she went back to work after having Leila caused the tax office to believe that her salary was twice what it was in reality and that she was incorrectly claiming Housing Benefit and tax credits.

Nine long months passed while she tried to resolve the problem, and before long the debt began to pile up. Two new credit cards and a bank loan were needed to cover the family's day-to-day living costs and keep up with the rental payments that she was now forced to pay as she was (incorrectly) deemed ineligible for Housing Benefit. She shut her mind to how she was going to pay back the money she owed because the priority was making sure that the family had a roof over their heads, and were fed and clothed. This 'tunnel vision' instinct overrode all other considerations.

The debts provided temporary respite but, inevitably, led to longer-term insecurity. Ruth's biggest fear was that they would lose their home, and so all of her energies were focused on preventing this scenario from unfolding. The consequence was that she steadily racked up arrears on all of her utility bills, and then defaulted on her loan repayments. This affected her credit rating, but it felt like a necessary evil.

The gnawing anxiety keeping Ruth awake at night shifted from how to pay the rent to how to hide the 'final demand' notices from the children. It always seemed to be the precise moment that Matthew headed out of the door to school that the postman would deliver his messages of misfortune.

One of the hardest aspects of Ruth's situation is that there was no network of family and friends to turn to when she was in dire financial straits. A common feature of many of our participants' stories is the lifeline that is offered by relatives who provide practical, emotional and financial help when times get tough. But for Ruth, this type of support has been notable by its absence.

What is striking, then, when she relates her story, is how appreciative she is of the small acts of kindness that she has received from the handful of people that she counts as friends, as well as staff at the local children's centre, who helped her to access the benefits that she was entitled to and signpost her to other services, such as the local food bank. It is easy to point out that "this is their job", but her gratitude towards those who have helped her is heartfelt and humbling. The food package that she was helped to get at her lowest ebb felt like a godsend.

There is evidence that more and more families are finding themselves in a similar situation to Ruth. The Trussell Trust (Loopstra and Lalor, 2017) reports that lone parents with children constitute the largest number of people receiving help from food banks, and more than a third of households using food banks have experienced an income shock in the past three months. Accepting a food package tends to be seen by users as an option of 'last resort' when other sources of support have been exhausted. Yet, food bank usage is currently at a record high (Loopstra and Lalor, 2017).

Ruth is conscious that her financial struggles have affected each of her three children in different ways. Despite wanting to shield all three of them from knowledge about what is going on, only Leila remains largely oblivious – partly because she has never known anything different, and partly because the family's earlier, more comfortable financial situation means that there are hand-me-down toys to play with and books to read. While Ruth is talking in the kitchen, Leila plays with some of these – a well-loved, threadbare bunny and a red Power Ranger – on the floor by our feet. She has warmed up a little and dared to edge away from the protection of her mother's skirt. Happily chatting away underneath our legs, it is hard to tell whether she is talking to – or on behalf of – her toys. Then a loud beep followed by a clicking noise cuts her game short as the electricity meter switches itself off and we are left in the semi-darkness while Ruth bustles into the hallway to turn it back on again with a newly topped up card. Leila is clearly unsettled by the interruption, and climbs back into the safety of her mother's arms, but the slightness of her reaction suggests that this has happened before.

The effect of Ruth's debt problems on Grace and Matthew are more clear cut. They are old enough to be aware of the difficulties that Ruth faces each month in making ends meet but also, importantly, they can remember how things used to be. They get their hair cut less often than they used to, for one, and they no longer get given money to spend on themselves. They are also aware of the stress that their mother is under, which sometimes causes her to snap at the smallest thing.

Matthew feels left out of his friends' conversations about the latest computer games that he can no longer afford to buy. But the biggest worry for him is the – thankfully, as yet unrealised – threat that he might have to stop going to football training. He is an able footballer, but the cost of training and transport to get there means that he is only able to continue because the football coach has stepped in to help, and a friend has lent him a bicycle for transport.

Last Christmas was "awful" because Ruth could not afford to buy anything beyond a token present for the children, but their appreciation for what they were given brought her to tears. There is a silver lining, perhaps, in the family learning about the cost of consumables, including, for example, how quickly the electricity meter whirrs around from £5 to zero. Never again will any of them pick something up in the supermarket without looking at the price tag.

In some ways, what is most striking about Ruth's story is that it is unremarkable. It is, perhaps, the archetypal journey into debt. A family that has been able to manage on a low – but not excessively low – earned income is thrown into disarray by a 'shock' to that income and no obvious alternative to credit. The ease with which Ruth's family slides from 'just about managing' to being in problematic debt suggests that very few low-income families are completely beyond the possibility of its clutches. Indeed, StepChange Debt Charity reported that 13 million people do not have enough savings to last a month if their income dropped by a quarter (de Santos, 2014). It is worrying, then, that changes to the benefits that working families are entitled to – specifically the two-child limit for Child Tax Credit that began to come into force in April 2017 – will make it harder for families like Ruth's in the future by limiting the amount that they can claim.[3]

Before I leave the house, I am faced with an ethical dilemma. Due to the later-than-anticipated start time to the interviews, it is now time for the children's evening meal. Ruth has made herself scarce while I am talking to Matthew but then she appears and asks if I would mind if she starts getting dinner ready. As she flits about, it is hard not to notice that her cupboards and fridge are bare. In my peripheral vision, I can see her cutting up an onion and boiling some rice. Dinner is going to be sparse. When I go to the toilet and use the last sheet of paper, my mind is made up. I bid my goodbyes and head straight to the supermarket where I buy a pizza, some salad, a few tins and some toilet paper. I knock on the door again, apologise, and hand over the bag of shopping. Ruth hugs me and we both burst into tears. I am fairly sure that I have breached some code of conduct – and we both promise not to tell anyone – but the humanity of the situation has overwhelmed me and I feel defiant. Some people believe that researchers should not alter the environment that they find themselves in for good or for ill. It is a small intervention, and it solves nothing in the longer term, but for Ruth and me, I think it is the right thing to do.

TWO

Isolation

Larissa Pople

Sitting on a cream sofa chatting to Stella in her sun-dappled lounge, with oak beams and low ceilings adding to the charm of the room, it is hard not to feel that this is a pretty idyllic setting.

Stella and her three children – 14-year-old George, six-year-old Maisie and three-year-old Callum – live in a picture-postcard village in an affluent part of the north of England where expensive, detached houses are interspersed with rows of terraced cottages along winding country lanes. Stella owns the diminutive-looking but spacious cottage that they live in with the help of a mortgage, and it feels like the kind of place to put down roots. Certainly this is their hope. But Stella tells me about a different reality – a story of financial problems and family break-up – which means that the longevity of their current living situation is far from assured.

Exactly a year before our interview, Stella's husband William upped and left with no warning. Although their relationship had been under strain, she thought that things were back on track, so his departure knocked her for six. In the run-up to him leaving, Stella found that she was using up what was left of her meagre savings to pay for food and essentials for the family. She assumed that her marriage was still intact and that one of them would be working again in the not-too-distant future (her husband had lost his job and she had stopped working to raise Maisie and Callum – see below). With the benefit of hindsight, she realises that this was the wrong assumption to make.

Until a few years earlier, the family were, on the face of it, pretty similar to many other middle-income families living in the UK, with one earner – in this case William – bringing in a decent wage of about £40,000 a year, and Stella's subsidiary income generated through her online 'upcycling' business adding a little extra to the pot. Resourcefulness combined with a little handiness with a sewing machine led Stella to work out that second-hand clothes picked up from charity shops could be jazzed up with beading, piping and sequins and sold on eBay for a reasonable profit margin. Thanks to careful juggling of childcare and income-generation activities, Stella and William were able to cover the everyday costs of family life with a bit left over for unforeseen expenses, such as when the roof sprung a leak.

They had fairly sizeable debts in addition to the mortgage, but these felt affordable and not out of proportion with the amount of money coming in. Not long after they moved into the cottage, Stella had taken out two bank loans: the first to buy furniture for their new home and the second to pay for them to get married. The loans were unsecured but – given their situation of relative financial stability – they felt manageable. In fact, even when Stella stopped working when Maisie and Callum were born, they were still able to manage with only William's income.

Their fortunes started to change when William lost his job. At first, the job loss did not feel like the end of the world. It was a major income shock, yes, but the redundancy pay-out was helpful in clearing some of the debts. However, with neither of them working and no regular income, the cost of everyday living came sharply into focus. Their mortgage lender agreed to a period of interest-only payments, but even these lower payments were not really affordable. The prospect of losing their home felt very real. Within the space of a few months, they had racked up four overdrafts, two credit cards and a bank loan. The monthly interest on these was substantial.

They pinned their hopes on William getting another job. However, after several months of scouring the job advertisements every day, and scraping together the petrol money needed to get to the occasional interview but still coming home empty-handed, William's hopes of finding a well-paid job faded. The interim solution was to take on shift work stacking shelves at a supermarket, while working a few hours a week for a local courier business. This earned him the equivalent of what he used to pay in tax. Meanwhile, Stella considered looking for a full-time job, but her 'pre-children' wage was a fraction of what William had been earning, and someone needed to look after the children. So she started the ad-hoc work that she could do from home again and fit around looking after the children: her online 'upcycling' business and a bit of childminding here and there.

Then misfortune struck again. William exacerbated an old injury in his shoulder, due, undoubtedly, to the heavy lifting and repetitive nature of the supermarket job, and so followed a period of several months of unemployment without any sick pay. It is not clear why William did not receive sick pay – Stella believes he must have been entitled to something – but he preferred to cut his losses and sever ties with the supermarket.

The family found themselves drifting apart, each disappearing into their own world. People deal with financial stress in different ways. Not being able to provide for the family hit William hard and he became depressed. This is not unusual. Research shows that unemployment and poor mental health often go hand in hand and that a 'scarring' effect means that wellbeing does not necessarily recover even when new employment is gained (Gedikli et al, 2017). In stark contrast to William's depressed inertia, however, Stella threw herself into meticulous organisation of the household finances, trying to retain some control of the increasingly bleak financial situation in a hive of nervous activity. She dutifully logged all of their debts, income and outgoings in her trusty spreadsheet. But as the interest on their debts snowballed, they reached a point when servicing them became increasingly untenable.

Their financial difficulties – and the differences in their coping strategies – were too great. After a year of trying to keep their heads above water, William walked out, and Stella was left alone to deal with the debts that had built up, the mortgage and three children, with no regular income. Not that William saw the debts as her sole responsibility, but without any material or psychological resources to help, in practice, it fell to Stella to organise them on behalf of them both.

The coalescence of unmanageable debt and relationship breakdown is not unique to Stella and William's story. Research points to a clear link between these two issues. Citizens Advice reports that clients who go to the organisation for debt advice are more likely than other clients to need support in other areas of their lives, such as with their relationships (Lane, 2016). Meanwhile a survey administered by the relationship support charity, Relate, found that almost a third (31%) of service users felt that debt had contributed to the breakdown of their relationship (Bradley and Marjoribanks, 2017). In a Children's Society's survey of children and their parents, more than half (57%) of parents with problematic debt felt that their relationship was under strain, and children were not in blissful ignorance of these problems. In the same survey, almost half (47%) of children living in households with problem debt said that a lack of money caused arguments in their family (The Children's Society and StepChange Debt Charity, 2014).

It was only at her lowest ebb that Stella was finally put in touch with an organisation that could set her up with a debt management plan. With the repayment plan in place, Stella felt in greater control of her debts. But even though her outgoings became more manageable, there was still a sense that she was just treading water, and that surviving on the money generated through her online business, which used to be a bonus to spend on treats for the children, was not realistic in the long term. Meanwhile, a big question mark hangs over the future of their living situation, and Stella fears that the patience of the mortgage company – to whom only interest payments had been paid for two years – will soon run thin.

One of the most striking features of their story is the stark contrast between their financial circumstances and those, apparently, of their neighbours. For Stella, the daily upheaval of counting the pennies to pay for the essentials is compounded by the feeling that they need to hide their financial struggles from all around them. While she frets about whether she has enough petrol to get the children to school and whether the car will pass its MOT, they are surrounded by tarmacked driveways and families with three cars to choose between. Other research supports the idea that social norms – whether others are in the same position – affect people's capacity to cope psychologically with the debt problems that they face. In areas like Stella's, where bankruptcies and mortgage repossessions are relatively rare, people with problem debt are more likely to have psychological difficulties than their counterparts in areas where evidence of debt problems is widespread (Gathergood, 2012).

There used to be family meetings to decide what the next family trip would entail, but these have fallen by the wayside. Stella has had to impose an amnesty on all non-essential car journeys, which means that George is no longer taken on cinema trips with his friends every fortnight, and Maisie and Callum have had to give up their after-school karate and trampolining clubs. "We don't do anything. We literally have no money to go to the cinema. We can't go swimming. We can't get the petrol to go anywhere."

All three children know not to ask for the treats and activities that they used to, but it is 14-year-old George who seems to have struggled the most. When Stella signed the children up for free school meals because she could no longer keep up the pretence that the family finances could cope without them, an awkwardness was introduced into George's relationships with his peers at school. Many of his classmates consider private tuition, expensive holidays and hand-outs of £50 to be the norm. In contrast, George uses his birthday money to 'splurge' on a pizza when a friend comes round after school. The social stigma associated with poverty can bring with it a thousand indignities. Pulling out his free school meal card at the school canteen checkout always makes George squirm because so few of his peers have one. The school provides financial support for school trips and grants for a uniform, but when his tutor bellows "Oh yeah, you're on pupil premium aren't you?" in front of the whole class, he wishes he could disappear into thin air.

The Children's Society's research on wellbeing shows that equality is often more important to children than wealth (see, for example, The Children's Society, 2016c). On average, wellbeing is highest for children who 'have about the same' amount of spending money as their friends. Children who have more or 'a bit less' than their friends have lower wellbeing, while wellbeing is lowest for those who have 'a lot less' than their friends. In an area like George's, children in a similar financial situation face a double whammy of poverty and inequality, with the pain of deprivation being magnified by comparisons with the comfortable lives of others.

George spends a lot of time in his bedroom playing games on the internet. He talks at length about the 'crew battles' that he plays online with friends – some of whom he knows, and others who he has met online – against other crews of players from across the globe. Violent video games may feature in the lives of many teenage boys, but in George's case, the line between fact and fiction is blurred because violence is increasingly a part of his real life as well. Head in hands, Stella tells me about the phone calls she has been getting from school. "George has been fighting, George has punched one of the other kids in the face, George has sworn at a dinner lady ... it's every other day."

"Yeah, I've got anger issues." These words seem easy for George to say, but he cannot easily articulate what brings on the anger. Some of the incidents are clearly money-related, including a couple of times when his friends have "taken the piss out of [him]" because he could not afford the £1 it costs to buy chips on the way home from school. There was also an incident with a dinner lady, who would not let him off 5p for a sandwich when he was short on cash one lunchtime. George admits that these incidents make him see red, and that he gets in trouble at school as a result.

Neither George nor Stella attributes his behaviour problems directly to the family's financial difficulties, but there is no doubt that increasing isolation from each other is a painful feature of their story. The constant backdrop to family life is "Mum working, always working", with the younger ones getting shouted at for being too noisy, and George being left to his own devices.

My interview with George also makes me think about the different dynamics that I have encountered during this research project. So many of the research participants I have talked with are female: mothers, mainly, and a number of teenage girls. The conversations tend to flow easily. For the most part, we meander around the topic effortlessly and I hardly need to consult the list of questions that I have prepared. I feel tuned into their body language and I know when to hold back, when to let an off-topic discussion runs its course, and when to gently bring things back. In interviews such as these, words are in abundance.

With George, however, it is a different story. I find myself relying heavily on my list of 'prompt' questions, grateful for all the pre-fieldwork preparation that I have done. Monosyllabic answers are his norm, and I struggle to draw out more in-depth reflections. I worry that he would rather not talk about this, or to me, and that the consent he has given to take part is not fully 'informed'. Yet every time I gently remind him that participation is voluntary and that consent is revocable – in other words, that he does not have to do this and can stop at any time – he is adamant that he wants to continue. Then, at the end, he tells me that he liked talking about it all. And I wonder how many times he has been asked what he thinks and feels before. I resolve to be more comfortable with fewer words, and with silence.

THREE

Loss

Sorcha Mahony

"You want to know about the debts then?", Alex asks, and with that his interview begins, with none of the opening conversational dance that often takes place, helping to make the process feel less formal, more relaxed. He is here to tell his story and he does so without fanfare, sitting in a dreary station café, competing with the clinking of crockery and intermittent train announcements. He avoids eye contact, jumps to the safe parts of his narrative and those at the forefront of his memory, back-filling the gaps and letting the absences speak louder than words.

Alex's debt story began in 2015. He was living with his wife and their two boys in a two-bedroomed house in the south east of England, where they had lived for seven years. He worked full time in a warehouse and his wife worked part time in a local supermarket. Their boys were aged eight and six. Joseph, the eldest, played the trumpet, which he had recently started learning at school, and Max, the youngest, was a dedicated Minecrafter and football enthusiast. Life was busy but 'pretty average' and financially they managed, just about. While the household income did not allow them to save anything, it helped to keep them afloat. With their joint monthly earnings of around £2,200, Child Benefit of around £135, tax credits of around

£100 and Housing Benefit of around £150 each month, they managed to pay their rent (£900 a month), the bills (including Council Tax, gas, electricity, water, the television package, mobile phones, school meals and trips and the boys' hobbies, which amounted to around £1,100 a month) and run a small second-hand car. Alex had two credit cards, his wife had some store cards, they had a catalogue account and an overdraft facility, and they considered these 'extras' necessary for living a life that felt far from extravagant but which enabled them to do more than just scrimp and struggle – to buy decent clothes, to upgrade the computer when necessary, to take the boys on holiday once a year, to go on the odd day trip or for a meal out, or to take the boys to the cinema at the weekend. "I mean we weren't living the high life or anything, just sort of getting by I suppose, with a few treats, you know?" With the £300 left over from the household income each month after paying the bills and other expenses, they made the minimum repayments to their creditors, and sometimes managed to pay the full amounts owed on the store cards. Things felt manageable, if tight. Debt – which Alex thinks probably amounted to "a few thousand odd" at the time – was an integral part of everyday life, woven into the fabric of their existence and not something they had reason to think about very much.

In the spring of 2015, all of this changed. Alex fell into a deep depression, was signed off work and was put on medication to reduce the suicidal thoughts that had begun to haunt him. His marriage broke down. Eventually his wife would move out, also suffering from profound psychological distress, heavily medicated and unable to work.

At first Alex does not speak of the catalyst for these events. He refers to a 'trauma' that the family experienced, but he avoids the specifics until in their absence they scream to be told. Only half way through our time together does he name the horror that made his world collapse, that made the will to live escape him for a while. In April 2015, Alex's youngest son, Max, died. It was sudden and unexpected, and the grief that followed was of a type and magnitude knowable only to parents who have lost a child. It bore down on Alex and his wife individually and it became wedged between them until it prised their marriage apart.

For a while the practicalities of life became a secondary concern. Alex does not remember eating or washing in the weeks after Max's death, only fitful sleep, a crushing weight on his chest and a slow constricting of the muscles in his throat, which left him gasping for breath in the night and unable to express his pain. His mother stepped in. She took Joseph to school and picked him up, and offered what little comfort she could while dealing herself with the loss of her youngest grandson.

Alex's wife moved out towards the end of the summer, her grief too much to bear, and Alex and Joseph began the slow, terrible process of learning to live alongside their loss. Alex returned to work and set about trying to sort out his finances, aware that the reduced rate of pay he had received while on compassionate leave was not sustainable, and increasingly uncomfortable with the pile of creditors' letters and payment demands that had been growing in his peripheral vision. Joseph became increasingly withdrawn and angry and Alex felt guilty that a lot of the time he was too distracted to give Joseph the attention he needed.

Although Alex returned to work full time and on full pay, the monthly household income was now reduced to a single salary – of £1,300 – and this was not enough to cover the outgoings, even with the existing benefits, which brought in approximately £350. He applied for additional support with housing costs but found himself stuck in a backlog of other requests, making do as best he could. He relied on the overdraft and credit cards to cover basic household expenses: "It used to be like the credit card for the extras, but then it turned to be like using them for the food and bills and that." He struggled to meet the cost of school for Joseph – the meals, the uniform, the trips, the after-school clubs and the trumpet lessons. His mother chipped in and his estranged wife contributed whenever she could, but Alex understood only too well the depth of her despair and her own financial precarity.

Alex could not put petrol in the car and relied more and more on his mother for lifts to and from work. He started to take Joseph to his mother's place every evening, where it was warmer and where they could have hot baths and meals, which they could not do at home. Alex was appreciative of his mother's help and ashamed that he had to rely on it. A friend came over, saw there was not much food in the fridge and offered to take Alex shopping. Alex was grateful and utterly humiliated. When Joseph asked if he could have some friends over after school, Alex said no – he could not afford to feed himself or Joseph properly, let alone other people's children. Alex's friend invited him to the pub to try to cheer him up and he laughed, at the simple impossibility of accepting the offer and at the bigger, messy awfulness of what was happening.

By early autumn, Alex's everyday life had come to be defined not only by Max's absence, his wife's departure and the psychological strains of single parenthood, but also by the relentless and seemingly fruitless struggle to make ends meet – the constant juggling of financial priorities referred to by many of our participants as 'robbing Peter to pay Paul' when the money coming in does not cover what is owed.

In late September, Alex received a letter from his landlord notifying him that he had missed the previous month's rent payment and that he needed to pay what was owed and ensure he kept up with payments in the future. Alex called the letting agent and explained the situation, asking for another month to get back on track – he felt sure that by then his application for increased Housing Benefit would have been processed. The landlord agreed, but also advised Alex that the rent would be going up at the start of the next financial year – the neighbourhood had started to gentrify and Alex's rent was now below the current market level for the local area.

Alex asked his employer for a raise and when his request was denied he asked if he could work extra hours, but was told that that would not be possible. So he sold his car for scrap and got £75, and sold a few pieces of furniture that he had inherited from his grandfather and got £160 – at considerable cost emotionally but nowhere near enough to cover the rent arrears let alone any of the other debts, which by now amounted to over £10,000.

Alex used the cash he had raised to pay the arrears on Joseph's school dinners and buy him a new pair of school shoes, as the ones he was wearing were two sizes too small. He also did a food shop for the first time in months, although he had stopped eating proper meals himself and lived on snacks and Joseph's leftovers. He considered moving to an area where rent would be lower, but that would entail moving away from his mother and starting Joseph in a new school, neither of which Alex judged to be in Joseph's best interests – his mother was a crucial source of support for them both and school was one of the few areas of stability in Joseph's life.

The weeks rolled on, they turned into months, and the chill of winter pierced the air outside and in. The gas meter remained empty and the electricity meter hovered in the emergency zone. Any cooking was done in the microwave. The house was damp and it was now impossible to dry clothes properly once they had been washed. In the gaps between work and looking after Joseph, Alex contacted as many of his creditors as he could, explaining again and again what had happened, trying to negotiate reduced monthly payments and reliving Max's death over and over. But mostly these endeavours were unsuccessful. Christmas came and went in a blur, the yawning chasm left by Max's absence stretched ever further open. Alex began to feel that despite his very best efforts and all the love in his heart, he was failing in his duty as a father.

In the new year, Alex and Joseph visited their doctor. She increased Alex's dosage of anti-depressants and prescribed sleeping tablets, and prescribed Joseph antibiotics to get rid of the chesty cough that had been lingering for weeks. She also diagnosed Joseph with trichotillomania – an impulse-control disorder defined by the urge to pull one's hair out, usually from the head but also from the eyebrows and eyelashes, and associated with stress, anxiety, guilt, shame and low self-esteem. The doctor also made two referrals: one for Joseph to an asthma clinic and the other for Alex to a food bank – a saving grace and the straw that broke him.

When they went home, Alex sat at the kitchen table and wept. Until now he had assumed that their financial situation was temporary – daunting, but one they could recover from. But it was becoming evident that this was unlikely; no amount of penny pinching or juggling was going to lift them out of the debt trap.

Two days after visiting the GP, Alex received another letter from his landlord, serving him notice to quit as he had not paid the arrears on his rent. He was to leave the property by the end of the month. It is not clear from Alex's interview whether he ever did receive the increased Housing Benefit payments he would have been entitled to, but even if he did, the changes to support with housing costs that came into force in 2013 as part of the government's welfare reform Bill (which entailed linking increases in Local Housing Allowance to the Consumer Price Index inflation rate, rather than the cost of local rents) could well have meant that any Housing Benefit entitlement would have failed to cover Alex's housing costs. In any case, Alex did not wait until the end of the month to move out. That evening he called his mother, borrowed her car and filled it with the belongings from the house that he and Joseph needed most – clothes, shoes, toiletries, the laptop, Joseph's school things, bike and trumpet, a box of Lego and some books.

They stayed with Alex's mother for a short time. She lived in a small one-bedroomed flat and Alex and Joseph slept in the living room – Alex on the floor and Joseph on the sofa, with their belongings scattered about the room. But Alex's mother had a partner who visited often and relationships quickly became strained as overcrowding, long-buried resentments and the persistence of grief came together in toxic combination. Three weeks after moving in, Alex came to blows with his mother's partner and that afternoon he contacted the local council to declare himself and Joseph homeless. That evening they moved into emergency accommodation – a hostel designed for, and for the most part inhabited by, single homeless men, many of whom suffered with alcohol and drug problems. They were told that they would be there for a few weeks, until something more suitable could be found. When I interviewed Alex, he and Joseph had been living in the hostel for five months. They were on a waiting list for a flat but they were not sure when they might be moving, or where they might end up.

When social researchers conduct interviews with people at vulnerable moments in their lives, we expect to encounter a certain level of emotional pain and we are usually prepared for it. But sometimes we find ourselves in at the deep end, confronted with a degree of anguish that tests our own emotional strength to its limits. Unlike the dedicated listening professions, whose supervisory structures allow – at least in theory – for the formal processing of psychological distress in those who bear witness to others' pain, in social research there is no profession-wide mechanism for dealing with the emotional toll that participant encounters can take. So we listen, swallow our pity, turn to our peers for support and channel our energies into documenting and sharing what we learn in the hope that it might help to shift attitudes and challenge the systems that give rise to hardship, or at least help to ameliorate some of the needless additional suffering experienced by people who have found themselves momentarily at a loss.

While our participants' experiences have varied and not all have known events as extreme as those of Alex and Joseph, loss is there in their stories, sometimes lurking in the shadows, sometimes front and centre. The loss of loved ones, of relationships, of health, of jobs – and following each of these, the loss of income – it runs throughout our debt data, but there is no clear place for it. There is insufficient room in the system to acknowledge it in a meaningful way, except perhaps for the allowances made for those with mental health problems.

The relationship between mental health problems and debt is widely recognised (see, for example, Lewis et al, 2017; Rethink Mental Illness, 2017; Mental Health Foundation, 2018), albeit that the direction of causality is difficult to establish. According to the Royal College of Psychiatrists (2017), one in four people with mental health problems is also in debt. But while there is some additional financial support available for those who find themselves at the very sharp end of severe mental health problems and problem debt (for example through Employment Support Allowance, the Personal Independence Payment or – for those who manage to hold down a job while haunted by the spectre of their loss – the disabled worker element of Working Tax Credit), the thresholds for eligibility tend to be extremely high and often people are unaware that they may be entitled. In any case, the losses that families suffer in their debt journeys don't always translate into easily identifiable and diagnosable mental health conditions, and so it is left to the third sector, to communities, to neighbours, to families and to individuals, to shape their own responses to the losses they know.

FOUR

Luxuries and necessities

Larissa Pople

"Let's talk about the debt then….", Faye shouts from the kitchen while she is boiling the kettle. Smiles are exchanged awkwardly with husband Dave, 15-year-old Sally and eight-year-old Archie while Faye bustles in with tea for us all and a packet of Tesco's-value chocolate biscuits. A pint-sized bundle of nervous energy, she vaults up onto the sofa, tucks her feet in underneath her and fixes me with a penetrating but friendly stare.

Faye has been in debt for most of her adult life. She took out her first loan at the age of 20 to pay for a "holiday with the girls", and while she was in the bank setting up the loan agreement, she found herself being talked into a credit card too. Marrying her first husband, Phil, a couple of years later, she has worked ever since, most recently as a kitchen assistant in a care home. But even with both Faye and Phil in full-time jobs – albeit low-wage ones that place them firmly in the 'low-income' bracket – they found themselves making regular use of catalogues, store cards and credit cards to pay for the things that they could not quite afford otherwise: a television, a stereo and some smart clothes for work. Over time the debts mounted up. The first loan they took out together was a consolidation loan to pay off the cards. Phil, who was an IT salesman, would sometimes receive a bonus around Christmas time, which would help to chip away at the total amount that they owed. Nevertheless, they never seemed to be able to wipe the slate completely clean.

When they divorced a few years later, Faye took out a bank loan to buy Phil out of the flat they had bought together, so that she and Sally, who was five years old at the time, could continue living there, with some extra to help with day-to-day costs. Within a matter of months, the loan was used up, so new lines of credit were needed, and even after selling the flat, Faye and Dave started their new life together saddled with debt. Faye describes a snowballing effect in which they found themselves taking out increasingly larger loans to cover the growing costs of servicing older debts.

There is the sense in Faye's story – which may, in part, be due to the nervous energy with which she tells it – that her debt has never really been manageable, even in the early days. Not that it feels senseless or gratuitous. Each new doorstep loan, credit card or catalogue account has paid for items that felt essential – food, clothes, "the electric" – as well as larger expenses including a down payment on a car and birthday presents for the children.

For low-income households, who spend a greater proportion of their incomes than wealthier households on food, accommodation and fuel costs, and increasingly so over time (JRF, 2015), credit is clearly an invaluable – sometimes the only – method of distributing the cost of items over a longer period of time. But as poorer households are likely to be constrained in the lending options available to them, and there are higher risks associated with lending to low-income borrowers, reliance on high-cost credit is an inevitable consequence. The result is that in addition to 'necessities' being proportionately more expensive for low-income households, 'luxuries' are often more expensive too.

The fundamental problem for Faye and Dave seems to be that they have never earned enough money to cover their day-to-day outgoings. It is largely a story of financial hardship, and a continuous cycle between poverty and debt. One dimension of this poverty – debt trap is that neither of them has savings that they can draw on. Faye apportions some of the blame for this to her parents who, she says, never talked about financial affairs or instilled in her the need to save. "We have no savings. I think that's what half our problem is."

She is right that savings can help households to cover unexpected costs or falls in income: one study found that a financial cushion of £1,000 almost halved the probability of being in problem debt (Surtees, 2015). But she is not alone in lacking savings to draw on: 49% of lower-income households (in this case, those with an income of between £200 and £300 per week) have no savings (Department for Work and Pensions, 2017); and low-income households are much less likely to take up government-run savings schemes such as Independent Savings Accounts (ISAs) (StepChange Debt Charity, 2015).

It is also hard to see where extra money for saving would come from, at least as their budget stands currently. The household monthly income is £1,500 (which includes Faye's monthly wage, tax credits and Child Benefit) and their carefully itemised outgoings – including the monthly repayments to their debtors – amount to £1,450. The small surplus has to cover unforeseen expenses such as the £5 contribution that is needed for Archie to go on the Southend beach trip with his class, and £3 for Sally's end-of-term disco. "That's the bread and milk right there, so she couldn't go, you know, which I felt terrible about…."

That said, Faye and Dave's house feels comfortable and inviting – like a home. As well as a stick insect in a glass box in the corner, the lounge houses a shelf of DVDs, some books, a functioning television and a few mismatched but not unattractive items of furniture. Faye explains that everything within sight has been given to them or acquired via Freecycle – an internet listing service that helps people give unwanted items to other people in their community for free – of which she is an avid user. Other big-ticket items have been accumulated over a period of several years.

Faye reflects on a time when she spent close to £300 on the children's Christmas present – a wooden playhouse for the garden, which felt like an enormous extravagance – although she knows they would have been happy with a fraction of that. "I went back to when I was a child. What would I have wanted if I was a child and my mum was still around? I would have loved a big, wooden playhouse. So we bought one."

Popular narratives around poverty and consumption can involve moralising about the things that people should or should not spend their money on. Would the playhouse fit into the latter category, and stoke up self-righteous anger about fecklessness? Or is a purchase such as this a carefully thought-out choice for someone who knows that there is little prospect of being able to afford these items within their means? Abhijit Banerjee – co-author of *Poor economics: A radical rethinking of the way to fight global poverty* (Banerjee and Duflo, 2011) – argues that it is logical for someone living in long-term poverty to ask themselves: 'If I feel that everything I've hoped for never worked, then what am I restraining myself for?' (Aitkenhead, 2012). It is difficult to exercise cast-iron impulse control if you know from bitter experience that your circumstances are unlikely to improve. From this perspective, prioritising the happiness and social inclusion of one's children, even when this means accepting indebtedness and its associated difficulties as a consequence, seems like a profoundly rational response.

Research suggests that low-income families tend to choose between two distinct approaches to consumption. Some, like Faye, opt for a credit route that enables their social participation, while others prefer to avoid debt at all costs and to forego material items and social activities that others would consider to be a 'normal' part of life. This may bring stability to their situation – and give them the moral upper hand in discussions of 'deserving and undeserving poor' – but it is tainted by the social exclusion and shame associated with being materially deprived.

Nowadays, Faye and Dave's household finances are managed with military precision, with income and outgoings detailed to the last penny. Faye is resourceful, taking Archie to the pet shop so he can look at the fish swimming around in their tanks instead of spending money on activities and entertainment. The biggest 'luxury' in their lives is on Fridays when both children get a packet of popcorn and some sweets. "We have one really short week and if madam is on, we don't buy milk and we buy her pads. You know? It's that sort of thing." I am not sure if I have heard correctly so I exchange looks with Faye and yes, she is talking about the expense of Sally's menstrual cycle, which has to be worked into the budget.

Spending money on activities for the children only happens when not participating would single them out. It breaks Faye's heart that she cannot buy art materials for Sally, and that Archie had to miss out on a friend's birthday party at 'Build-a-Bear' because she was not sure if the bear would be paid for or not. Her greatest desire is to have a little bit of money left over once all of the careful budgeting has been done to be able to treat the family to a trip to the cinema or swimming.

Without being familiar with the minutiae of the family's indebtedness, Sally is aware that the family's finances are "being stretched quite far" and that means adjusting her expectations downwards. It is a case of delaying gratification, or not asking at all. Faye is grateful for the maturity and understanding that Sally shows when new school shoes or a new pair of glasses cannot be bought straight away as they might once have been. There is a lot of "waiting" – sometimes until the end of the month, sometimes indefinitely. Sally says:

'I've sort of stopped asking for my art supplies as well now. Because it's like as much as I like to do my arts and crafts, we can't really afford it now so you sort of– I would rather the family get the food and necessities rather than me get my own things for my benefit. Because I feel like I'm being selfish.'

But for Sally, the harshest aspect of their financial deprivation is a gradual withdrawal from social interactions outside of the immediate family. Some of Sally's friends are in a similar financial situation, but others go out regularly, which leaves her feeling "segregated" and "different". Sally also sorely misses going on family trips. Nowadays the most they will do as a family is go for a walk on the common nearby. "There's an ice cream van down there and we will sometimes buy one for Archie but the rest of us are like 'Better not have an ice cream, because....'."

The solution to the family's current problems is a debt management scheme, which means that – in the short term at least – they will be unable to take out further credit. But for Faye, this is a help, not a hindrance. In her view, credit is far too easily accessible. Even Sally, who is yet to turn 18 and is still in full-time education, receives credit card offers through the post regularly. It takes strong resolve – or bitter experience – to resist such temptation. But Faye is determined for her children not to replicate her mistakes: "I know it's my own stupid fault I'm in this situation. But on the other hand I think that the future generation needs to be educated far more than what I was…. There's no 'If you do this, this is what will happen'."

There is some evidence that financial education can help, especially if it is adapted to the unique circumstances and strengths of the person in question (Consumer Financial Protection Bureau, 2016). The research in this area suggests that financial education needs to move beyond simply increasing people's knowledge *about* financial concepts, to teaching action-based strategies and shifting the emphasis from knowledge to behaviour by providing people with the opportunity to practise the skills they have learned (Spencer et al, 2015). But financial education is only part of the answer. For Faye and Dave, the challenges of bringing up a family on a low-income – and coping with unexpected income shocks and additional expenditure along the way – cannot be overstated. The monthly ordeal of balancing the books, learned through experience of the perils of the alternative, is a story of endless deprivation and sacrifice. Faye says: "I don't want millions. I would be happy with a little pot and the kids could go: 'Mum, I want to go to the pictures.' There you go. 'Mum, I need shoes.' Go on then."

FIVE

Who cares?

Sorcha Mahony

"Hello?" – a monotone voice, a noise like sandpaper at the other end of the line, then silence. "Steven?", I ask, concerned that I have got the wrong number or that I am calling at the wrong time. "Yeah?" And so we start like this, in monosyllables, and I find myself wishing Steven had agreed to meet in person where I imagine conversational props and opportunities to connect might have been more readily available. Telephone interviews can be so impersonal.

Steven coughs and clears his throat frequently, and he speaks so fast that I have to ask him to repeat himself often. But we judder along for the next hour or so, awkwardly, stiltedly, and he tells his story – ostensibly one of problem debt, but more fundamentally one of growing up without the support necessary to weather even the smallest of financial storms.

Until the age of six, Steven had been living with his mother, father and older brother, but his parents' marriage was an unhappy one and around the time of his seventh birthday his father left. Shortly afterwards, his mother's new partner moved in, bringing a host of addictions and a violent streak into the family home. Steven's mother, now dealing with her own addictions and ill-health, began to neglect her children and they were placed with a foster family – an arrangement intended to be temporary but one that became a defining feature of Steven's childhood.

Steven and his brother moved from one foster family to another, and when Steven was 10, after numerous failed placements, the boys were split up; they fought endlessly and when Steven was hospitalised after his collar bone was broken by his brother, a decision was made to place them with different families.

Over the next four years, Steven lived with 12 foster carers. When he was 14 he was moved into a residential care home – a last resort for young people who have not settled in family-based care. At the age of 17, Steven left the care home and stayed in a respite unit for a few months before moving into a hostel. After a year in the hostel he moved into accommodation designed to bridge the gap between institutional care and independent living – a half-way house of sorts. At the age of 19, he was placed in a council flat by himself – his introduction to 'independent living'. Steven has been in the flat for a year, his only company being the strange noises from his upstairs neighbour 'Dr Spook' and a pigeon that coos incessantly from the windowsill outside his bedroom.

Steven has had a few short-term jobs: as a pot-washer in the kitchen of a local pub, as a labourer in a garden centre, as a coffee shop assistant and as a shelf-stacker in a supermarket. But his placements never seem to work out. He shows up every day and works as hard as he can, but always seems to come away from the trial periods with a friendly pat on the back and no job. He looked into the possibility of studying again but could not afford the fees, felt overwhelmed by the bureaucracy entailed in applying for the funding he was probably entitled to, and anyway the nearest college to offer the horticultural course he was interested in entailed a 50-mile round trip, four times a week. He has just started receiving around £58 a week in Jobseeker's Allowance (JSA) and is looking for work.

A few months after Steven began living independently, he decided to buy a bike so that he would not be so constrained by the cost of travel in the local area and would not feel so isolated from the friends he had made at the hostel. His voice is barely a whisper as he explains how bored he gets in the flat by himself and I realise how hard it is for him, not only to go for days on end without company, but also to tell this to a stranger. He mumbles that he did not have the money to buy a bike, so instead of paying his electricity bill (which was around £120 a month as the flat did not have a gas supply and used electric storage heaters, which were expensive to run), he used his next JSA payment to buy a pack of vintage football cards, which he listed on eBay with a view to making a profit so that he could pay his bills *and* get a bike.

Nobody bid. Instead of making money, Steven was left with a stack of unwanted football cards, a debt to the energy company and no bike. "I messed that up," he mumbles. The following fortnight's JSA payment did not allow him to pay the electricity bill and buy food and toiletries, so Steven borrowed from a payday loan company so that he could do both. But a month went by and he found that he could not repay the loan and the interest he had been charged, so he requested more time. The loan company agreed and gave him another month, as well as extra interest and an additional fee for the rollover. Steven's attempts to find a job were still not paying off, so he touted around for cash-in-hand work, but his efforts only yielded a day's work helping a friend move, which brought in £30 – enough to pay for a grocery shop, but not to repay the loan. His JSA payments seemed to disappear on food, travel, credit for his phone and household bills, and he worried. He worried about what the loan company would do, about the extra charges he would incur, and more generally about his capacity to manage independently. By the end of the second month, Steven was eating little and trying not to use the electricity in the flat. He told himself he should be able to manage and went over and over his budget to see where he could squeeze things a bit tighter.

In the stress of it all, Steven missed a payment for his Council Tax. While he received support with his Council Tax bill, he was still liable to pay a proportion of it, and he forgot a monthly instalment (cuts to Council Tax Benefit mean that most councils no longer offer full help with Council Tax). The local authority wrote to him, first giving him a week to pay, then withdrawing the option to pay by instalments and threatening to take him to court and charge him legal fees. He called the council to try to negotiate a repayment scheme, asking to reinstate the option of paying by instalments, but his request was refused. He asked to speak to a manager but was told that a manager was not available. He requested a call-back and the phone went dead.

"I'll be honest with you," Steven says, "I did smash some things up like," and he describes how he picked up the microwave after he got off the phone and dropped it on the kitchen floor in a fit of anger. It's painful to listen as he mutters, clears his throat and speaks almost apologetically about being pushed to the brink, not listened to, not taken seriously. "They just saw me in that stereotypical way, like 'he's just caned his money, it's his fault'."

Steven was already sleeping and eating badly and now developed a headache that woke him in the morning, stayed with him most of the day and accompanied him to bed at night. He decided to pay off the Council Tax bill as a matter of urgency, as he did not want to go to court – and pay for the privilege – and to sort out the payday loan repayment later. So with his next few JSA payments he rid himself of the Council Tax debt and of the capacity to feed himself properly. Over the next few months, Steven continued to make do with little in the way of material resources, eking out his toiletries, shopping in the clearance section of the supermarket and avoiding the use of electricity in the flat. Instead – when it was cold – he wore all of the jumpers in his wardrobe and every pair of socks he owned during the day, and slept in his clothes and outerwear as well as pyjamas at night. He hustled for odd jobs that paid cash in hand through friends and acquaintances, the informal economy his only hope of raising enough money to pay off the payday loan.

Steven is almost back on track with his finances now. He says that in another few weeks he will have paid off the loan, and he is in the clear with his electricity account. He does owe money again for his Council Tax, as it is April and he has received his first bill of the new financial year, but that will have to wait until the end of the week when his JSA comes through.

When I ask what might have helped him through the rough times, Steven says he would have liked an adult to advocate on his behalf, and I realise that he occupies a strange, liminal space in the popular imagination – ostensibly an adult and assuming the independence this entails, yet without the resources necessary to make a success of independent living. While in care he had received training designed to prepare him for independence, including around finances and managing money, but it was focused on budgeting and, as Steven says, "there's only so many times you can redo a budget if there's not enough money in it".

Our time is nearly up and I ask Steven to put some figures to his debts – until now he has talked, bashfully but in some detail, about many aspects of his life and financial struggles, but not about how much he actually owed to whom. He says that the amount has fluctuated over time, but that at their height his combined debts – on the payday loan and the Council Tax – reached a total of £250 and that he currently owes £30 on his Council Tax again. He talks about how stressful it is, how worried he feels about balancing everything, about bailiffs turning up at his door, and about ending up in court.

I have to double-check these figures. Somehow, a total debt of £250 and a current debt of £30 seem incommensurate with the effect they have had on him – the sleepless nights, the persistent headache, the poor diet, the lack of sleep and the anger. But I heard right: the most he ever owed was £250 and he has one outstanding payment to make to the local authority of £30.

The interview finishes, we hang up and I start to question whether Steven really belongs in our research sample; whether he can properly be understood to be experiencing 'problem' debt. But the more I think about it, and the more people I go on to encounter whose debts also amount to relatively little in monetary terms yet cause considerable stress, the clearer it becomes that they are telling us something simple yet crucial. They signify – among many other things – how important it is to have social networks you can draw on in times of need, how profoundly dependent we are on those networks, especially informal, kin-based ones, for access to resources and how, if these are patchy or fall away altogether, people are so exposed, in economic and related psychological terms.

It is easy to forget this fundamental dependency and the paradoxical way it enables us to function as 'independent' adults. It is so much a part of the story of our achievements – and so contrary to the pervasive and interrelated neoliberal discourses of independence and personal responsibility – that it seems to have become invisible. All the myriad ways that close friends and family help us, providing what sociologists call financial, social and cultural capital, are so easily forgotten in the scramble for recognition as successful, independent adults. We might even feel inclined to think of ourselves as architects of our own destiny, sinking or swimming in a sea of potential achievements by virtue of our hard work alone.

But Steven knows differently. While he might be *the* archetypal embodiment of the neoliberal subject, he knows that, in reality, people accomplish success and independence by being able to depend on others in the first place, and that without being able to, the holy grail of financial security remains elusive to all but a very few. While he has a network of sorts, it is not one he can rely on. It is made up of friends whose company he enjoys but whose own fortunes are much like his, social workers who Steven says are "always on training courses or long-term sick", and project workers who get their funding removed, find jobs elsewhere or take up other professions. He is in contact with one of his previous foster families but does not feel able to turn to them for financial assistance, and is not in touch with his brother, father or extended family. He has been in contact with his birth mother, but has not spoken to her since she recently refused to lend him £10 to put credit on his phone and get a take-away. Again, he mutters and stumbles over his words as he explains:

'I had a row with my mum and basically I said to her: "Look I've not eaten all day, can you just lend me some money so I can go out and get something to eat?" And she was like "no". She's a bit funny like that, yeah. She said "no" anyway and all I had that evening was water. Yeah, it's not brilliant … I used to get free sarnies from the café where she worked, but that stopped.'

And Steven's voice trails off as he remarks: "She hates me."

Around 10,000 young people aged 16–18 leave care each year in England (NAO, 2015). In 2017, local authorities around the country supported 37,720 care leavers aged 19–21 (Department for Education, 2017) and can expect to support many more in 2018 as councils' responsibilities towards those leaving care are extended to the age of 25 under the Children and Social Work Act 2017. Although many care leavers go on to achieve remarkable things, those who have been in care are a vulnerable group, with their health, housing, education and employment outcomes severely compromised compared with others (NAO, 2015). With no family to support them to the degree required, and with local authorities stepping away in their role as corporate parents at a set age, the transition to adulthood can be a difficult, lonely and costly one. Financial problems and debt are pressing issues for some: in their research, the Centre for Social Justice (2015) found that 57% of young people leaving care find it difficult managing money and avoiding debt.

Since 2015, The Children's Society has been lobbying for care leavers to be exempt from paying Council Tax until they are 25 years old, in order to make the move into independent living easier, to help prevent money problems taking root and in recognition that young people who have grown up within a family environment rely on support from their parents for increasing lengths of time (Become, 2018). So far around 60 councils around the country have voluntarily exempted care leavers from paying Council Tax. Unfortunately, Steven does not live in one of the local authority areas that has chosen to take such progressive action.

The way Steven chose to share his debt story is interesting. For many qualitative social researchers, there is an assumption that interviewing participants in person is *de facto* preferable to interviewing them over the phone. While the latter may be necessary in some circumstances, say for practical or logistical reasons, it tends to be seen as a pale approximation of the real thing, with the phone being an obstacle in the way of a more personal, authentic encounter. But for some people, this is precisely why telephone interviews work: they can be so impersonal. And in this they allow those who might otherwise find it impossible, to tell the stories that bring pain or shame, that pull into sharp focus the fact that they have no one who cares enough to lend them a tenner and not mind too much when they pay it back.

SIX

The elephant in the room/consumerism

Larissa Pople

'I come from a very poor background, you know, which has never bothered me because I learnt that you get what you're given. Mum made my school jumpers and things like that. It didn't bother me. But when it came to getting married I thought: "What do we do?" We were working, so she said: "Why don't we get a bank loan?" So I did. I borrowed £2,000. A lot of money in them days, back then. It paid for the wedding, the honeymoon and other bits and pieces.'

Kevin's argument seems reasonable. Here is someone who has been brought up with a philosophy of living within your means, however meagre those are, and with an understanding and acceptance of poverty defining every family decision that is made; but someone who, when it comes to pivotal moments such as moving out of the family home, getting married and starting a family, starts to wonder what is expected of him and his wife. Should they conform to societal expectations to fly the nest and set up as an independent, self-sufficient new family unit, which is in reality beyond their means? Or is it better to choose the path that society deems morally righteous of not becoming indebted, even when this brings with it the threat of social exclusion? It is hard not to feel that they are damned if they do and damned if they don't.

When Kevin and Jill first discussed getting married, neither had family money to draw on, so the only option they felt they had was to take out a loan. Both were working at the time – Jill full time as a nurse and Kevin part time in a local shop – so from a creditor's point of view, they ticked all the boxes. Indeed, for a 'honeymoon' period – an apt phrase in their case – they were able to cover the loan repayments fairly comfortably, and they did not doubt that they had made the right decision. But then Jill fell pregnant with Katy, and Sarah five years later, and the reality of bringing up young children in a low-wage family hit home. When Katy was six months old, Jill went back to her old job, but her wage only just covered the cost of childcare. Kevin's insubstantial income was expected to stretch to the rest. It fell short by a long shot, not helped by the monthly payments they were making to repay the loan.

At this point, having already been introduced to the world of credit, the solution seemed straightforward. New debts followed easily – catalogues, hire purchase and several doorstep loans. Unlike the first loan, which they discussed at length, agonising over every detail and potential consequence, new lines of credit were taken on without much thought. In Kevin and Jill's accounts of how they ended up with problem debt, there is a tacit acceptance that they are trapped in a vicious cycle of poverty and debt. Debt is their ticket out of the social exclusion that accompanies poverty. Yet ironically it also serves to exclude them further.

Kevin and Jill do not dwell on the reasons why they have little contact with their respective families, and there is much left unsaid. In other situations, we have been told about the pivotal role that grandparents, aunts, uncles and older siblings play in subsidising household incomes, paying for unforeseen, one-off expenses and making 'in-kind' contributions such as providing regular childcare. But instead of counting on emotional and practical support within the family, Kevin and Jill found they had to escalate all otherwise unaffordable, material demands to a shopping list of 'items to buy on credit'.

Along the way, this shopping list started to include not just items that are essential for survival but a few, more expensive items – a computer, a car on hire purchase. And why shouldn't they? Despite being frowned upon by some, these items are widely agreed to be social necessities (Main and Pople, 2011). Besides, a vast marketing industry devises ingenious strategies to persuade people to part with their money, and all but a tiny proportion of the population participate in this persuasion. Every day, Kevin and Jill's letterbox is full of unsolicited catalogues and offers of credit, and the television advertises the toys that Katy and Sarah's friends are raving about at school. When Katy was bought a scooter for her sixth birthday, and Sarah a second-hand Xbox when she was 10, the family were not just buying possessions that they could ill afford, but forms of cultural capital that they could not afford to be without.

Sadly, for Sarah, now aged 13, the prospect of fitting in with her peers at school is a pipe dream, always just beyond reach. When she talks about her friends at school, stuttering, eyes fixed on a hole in the carpet, it is all too clear that she has not been able to pull the wool over their eyes. While Kevin is "chuffed to bits" with the box of computer games that he "bought for a tenner at a car-boot sale", at school the conversation has moved onto the latest Fifa game and the Nike Huaraches that some of the children are wearing. Sarah cannot hope to keep up with these dizzying heights of consumption.

Sarah feels unpopular and excluded at school. She draws comfort from a couple of friendships that she has with children who are in a similar financial situation to herself, but counts very few people as friends. Bullying is a painful feature of everyday life. She describes one incident in which she was beaten up by a group of children, and then had to relive the experience because someone had videoed the incident and shared it on social media.

Some might think of the possessions that Sarah wishes she had – as well as the car and computer that her parents bought on credit – as 'luxuries', but they are items that the vast majority of the population have. In a Children's Society's survey of 10- to 13-year-olds in England, 94% of children said that they had a computer, and 89% said that they had a family car (Rees and Main, 2015). Lacking these items singles a family out visibly as deprived, as they are widely enjoyed by the society in which they belong. Indeed, this is Townsend's (1979) definition of poverty. If families like theirs are expected not to spend money on goods and activities that most people consider to be part of ordinary living, then the ethics of advertising strategies that target them should be brought into question.

Eventually, Kevin and Jill had to get rid of their car when it became financially impracticable to maintain it. Friends occasionally help them out by driving them to the supermarket, but ever since they have been carless, they have not been able to drive to church. Religion is important to the family, so on Sundays they take two buses to church and three buses back via Lidl so that they can do their weekly grocery shop on the way home. The cost of the round trip is almost equivalent to the cost of a taxi. It would be much cheaper to drive. Having a car is costly, but not having one can be more so.

The family's journey into problematic debt is not just about a low-wage couple trying to keep up with the treadmill of consumerism. This is the skeletal structure of their story; but the flesh and blood are to be found in other details, such as the Type II diabetes that forced Jill to stop working when both girls were still at primary school. Neither Jill nor Kevin thought that this is where they would end up, but who factors illness and disability into their life plans?

Kevin muses about what might have helped them. As council tenants, there was a period of time after Katy turned 16 when they might have been able to move to a larger, three-bedroomed house had they pursued this. But at the time their energy was taken up with Jill's illness and the increasingly problematic debt situation, and by the time they realised that they were entitled to separate bedrooms for the girls, the window of opportunity had passed and Katy had moved out (temporarily, as it turns out) to live at her boyfriend Kai's house.

Now full-grown adults in the eyes of the benefits system, Katy and Kai are living in Kevin and Jill's lounge and – to Kevin and Jill's delight

– there is a grandchild on the way. I get mixed messages about how the current set-up is working for all involved. Kevin argues, a bit too emphatically, that he would not have it any other way, but I get the impression that Sarah is not overly keen on having Kai in residence, and I cannot help but wonder whether Sarah's self-confessed retreat into her bedroom where she spends "five hours a day on her Xbox" is related. Now there are five voices arguing over what programme to watch on the television, and Sarah does not strike me as the loudest voice in this particular lounge.

Towards the end of the interview, Kevin says that he is considering taking out another loan to pay for a deposit and two months' rent so that Katy and Kai can move out of their lounge and into their own place. Ideally, he would get a loan large enough to stretch to a television too, as that is what he would have wanted from his own parents. His reasoning sounds both fantastical and logical. Once you accept that many of 'life's key moments' are beyond your pocket and always will be, but that you can purchase them (at a premium) on credit, why stop at one?

On the way home from this interview, when I am offloading my thoughts uncensored to Sorcha – the only other person who will ever know who this family is – we talk about the politics of representation and the thorny issue of what to include and what to omit from research outputs. We are all too aware of the popular narratives around the 'deserving' and 'undeserving', and do not want to add kindling to the fire of vitriol that is often aimed at those deemed morally irresponsible for choosing debt over social exclusion. At the same time, their story needs to be told. It is a story about the things we are encouraged to value and told we should be able to access. Getting married, having children and providing them with the things that other children have – that's not just for the rich: that's for all of us, right?

SEVEN

Guilt

Larissa Pople

"You like bhaji? And chai?", Seeta asks, sliding some home-made balls of bhaji mixture into the oil and pouring chai into a cup. In situations such as these, social researchers know that what they must do is gracefully accept the gift. These are the rules of engagement. It may even iron out some of the imbalances of power that can exist between researcher and participant. Nonetheless, it is hard not to feel a little discomfited that Seeta is sharing what little food she has.

Seeta and Vijay live with their two younger daughters, Salilah and Kiran, in a three-bedroomed duplex in a high-rise block close to Birmingham city centre. Their two older sons, who are in their early 20s, have left home and are living in bedsits close by. The sparsely decorated lounge looks out across a small communal strip of grass to a busy road, which merges with one of the main arteries into Birmingham a few hundred yards away. It is not beautiful, but it is comfortable, and what is lacking in furniture is made up for in the tantalising smells of cooking and the warmth of Seeta's welcome.

Their debt story starts in the same way as many others. A major income shock – in this case, the collapse of the family business – threw their finances into disarray. About 20 years previously, they had set up their own taxi business, with Vijay driving and Seeta handling the phones. Sometimes other relatives were involved in the business as drivers, and it worked well to keep the business in the family because the workload was unpredictable. When they were busy – for instance, if there was a big conference or concert on in the city centre – they could call on numerous relatives as additional drivers at short notice. But there was never an expectation of a guaranteed level of work, which was helpful because it was hard to know how much business they would have on a given day, week or month.

Most of their custom involved journeys to and from the airport, so things became difficult when the recession affected the number of people flying. People were just not travelling by plane in the same numbers as before. Demand slowed over a number of years until eventually the business collapsed. In the immediate aftermath, Vijay took on a job at a recycling centre, desperate to bring in an income and keep the family above the breadline. But the manual work, which he was not used to, took its toll on him. One hot day in July, he passed out next to one of the recycling containers. He had had a mini-stroke, and that was that as far as Seeta was concerned. "It's a young man's game," she explains to me. Around the same time, Seeta started working part time in the kitchen of a local primary school, earning about £9,000 a year, but her monthly wage was small change in comparison with what the taxi firm used to make.

With no savings to help, they turned to mail-order catalogues, doorstep loans and payday loans to pay for everyday living. For a number of years, Seeta and Vijay kept up with their repayments as best they could, but over time, increasingly larger debts were needed. At one point, they paid a debt management company to help manage their debts, but this was costly. Eventually, they reached breaking point. Bursting into tears on the telephone one day to a member of staff at one of the catalogues they owed money to, Seeta found herself talking to a sympathetic ear and she was referred to a debt charity. The best option in their case turned out to be bankruptcy. Not what they envisaged as erstwhile business owners, but preferable to the alternative.

As for many of our participants, it seems incongruous that Seeta and Vijay relied on high-cost credit for such a long period of time when more affordable credit must have been available. A lack of knowledge about lower-cost alternatives is likely part of the explanation. Various measures have been recommended to increase the flow of information to consumers to help them choose lower-cost credit (CMA, 2015). However, research shows that high-cost credit has become increasingly prevalent in recent years (StepChange Debt Charity, 2015), and that low-income households turn to high-cost credit for a number of reasons, including personal preference (Hartfree and Collard, 2014). With a credit history that is chequered thanks to the demise of their business, Seeta and Vijay are unable to access some of the mainstream credit options that others can draw on, including bank loans, overdrafts and credit cards. Furthermore, government-provided grants and interest-free loans that in the past might have been available to help families like theirs have been cut back. Between 2010–11 and 2015–16, central government stopped providing crisis loans, devolved 'local welfare provision' to councils and reduced its core funding by an estimated 37% (NAO, 2016).

However, in Seeta and Vijay's case, the role of personal choice cannot be disregarded. High-cost credit suited them, at least at the point of access, because it was easy to obtain and could be acquired from the comfort of their own home away from prying eyes. There was also an element of denial, and a belief that on each occasion they only need to borrow a small sum of money for a short time period. In practice, of course, that was rarely how things transpired.

"The worst thing about the debt is how it has affected family life," explains Seeta. They used to spend almost every weekend visiting relatives or hosting family gatherings at their flat, but now these are memories of happier times. Every day on the way home from school, Salilah and Kiran used to get a pound coin each to spend at their uncle's shop on snacks and a drink, and he would let their money stretch to more than face value with a wink and a "Shh, don't tell your dad." Seeta gives the impression that their extended family would happily continue these traditions without reciprocity, but Vijay is proud and will not accept 'charity', even from family.

From time to time, when it is one of the children's birthdays or if an essential household appliance breaks down, Seeta asks one of her aunts for help without telling Vijay. But these requests are few and far between. Besides, it is the social interactions rather the financial help that Seeta misses the most. When the girls were little, they spent so much time with their cousins that they felt like siblings. Seeta longs to host the whole family like they used to. But Vijay is resolute. So the girls have not seen their cousins in more than a year. And Seeta is wracked with guilt.

Guilt is a recurrent theme in their story: guilt that they can no longer give their children the things that their cousins have; guilt – and shame – that they used to be able to supplement the incomes of their extended family through their business, and now they cannot even afford to invite them over for food; guilt about the debt; guilt about every item in their house that is not essential for survival.

Blaming themselves for the predicament that they find themselves in, Seeta and Vijay seem to have internalised negative stereotypes of irresponsibility, and become unwitting agents of their own humiliation.

Seeta is at great pains to explain that the reason they have a Sky package is because – in comparison with other forms of entertainment – it is relatively cheap and can be enjoyed by the whole family.

> 'We've got the full package on Sky, even though we've talked to them and they've helped reduce down the payments for us. Because we don't do anything. We literally have no money to go anywhere. We don't have the car any more. But we couldn't pay for the petrol anyway.'

It is a sound argument, but the guilt seeps into her voice as she sets it out.

On the face of it, Salilah and Kiran – now aged 13 and 11 – have similar material items to their peers. There is a family computer – bought during more prosperous times, Seeta is keen to point out –

that the girls can use for homework, and which their older brothers sometimes come round to use if they need to fill in online applications for jobs or benefits. At secondary school, all the children have their own phones, and Salilah is no different as she has Vijay's old phone. But it is cracked and only works if it is plugged into the charger. Seeta has put £1 credit on it in case of an 'emergency' or if Salilah needs to call home for any reason, although it is hard to envisage how this will work in a real emergency if it needs to be hardwired to a source of electricity.

Salilah's older brothers are both looking for work, but their job search has been tortuous, and when they call home from time to time asking for money for food or electricity, Seeta and Vijay feel obliged to help, even though they have so little money of their own. "They still turn to us. And, being family, we feel obliged to support them." When asked why they are not still living at home with them, Seeta clearly does not want to talk about it. One of the loans they took out was to help the older two children when they moved out.

It is half past five by the time I leave. A dismal day in mid-January, it is pretty much pitch black outside. Seeta insists on following me out into the darkness and pointing me in the right direction. She wants to walk me to my car, but with all the firmness I can muster, I explain that the car is just around the corner and I'll be fine. I am relieved that I am parked three whole streets away, which was an intentional ploy to ensure that my first encounter with Seeta is not associated with the car I am driving. It may be tempting to draw comfort from the obvious differences in Seeta's life and my own by a process of 'othering', but instead my dominant feeling is guilt. Guilt again, but in this case, my guilt about the privilege I have in my life. If asked, I would hasten to point out that the car is my partner's and not mine, but first impressions count and I do not want this to define the interactions between us.

EIGHT

The Others

Sorcha Mahony

While some of our participants convey a strong sense of guilt around the experience of problem debt, internalising the negative stereotypes and blaming themselves for 'their' predicaments, others adopt an alternative response to the financial difficulties they encounter. They work hard to distance themselves from the pejorative stereotypes by invoking an imaginary other that fits the mould of the *immorally indebted* and constructing themselves in opposition to it – as indebted, yes, but for morally justifiable reasons. The participants who engage in this psychosocial process of othering do so to varying degrees. Where it exists it is sometimes quite subtle, unwittingly revealed in a slip of the tongue or suggested in the odd passing comment. But for a few, like the Other family, it seems to permeate the entire research encounter – the particular way they take control of the opening conversation, how they frame their responses to our questions and how they welcome us into their homes.

The Other family is a family of three living in a housing estate in the west of England, where they have lived for the past few years in a well-kept, pre-fab, three-bedroomed house. I arrive late for our meeting, having got lost on the way from the train station, and Mrs

Other stands on the door step waving frantically as I head up the path. "Thank God for that, I thought something had happened, there's some well-dodgy people around here," she says, steering me through the front door and glancing both ways as she closes it behind her. "You walked?" she asks incredulously and then: "Sorry, I'm Sally. You should have got a cab, it's not safe." A girl and boy appear at the top of the stairs and Sally instructs them to come down and say a proper hello, and she introduces 11-year-old Caitlyn and seven-year-old Damian, who stand there poking and pinching each other before racing back upstairs, scrambling to get up first until Caitlyn slaps Damian on the forehead and pushes past him to the top.

Sally and I stand at the kitchen counter and I'm ready to start the interview preamble but she has not finished talking about the area or the kind of people it attracts, explaining that she does not like living there but has little choice as she "got into a bit of a financial pickle" in the past, which meant she had to move, and the current property was all that was available in her price range, close enough to Caitlyn and Damian's schools. She talks at length of the drug users, the alcoholics and the motorbike racers whose engine revving provides the unwelcome soundscape to their daily lives, of the pyromaniacs whose night-time antics usually result in at least one visit from the fire brigade each month, and of the unruly children on the estate. "It's basically where the undesirables live," she says, summing up with a laugh: "We just keep to ourselves really."

To have participants appropriate the beginning of an interview is not uncommon. While most remain focused on the topic and questions at hand, some seem to use the opportunity to offload about apparently unrelated issues, to talk about the things that are on their mind and have sometimes been there a while – a traumatic experience of childbirth, a feud with a neighbour, a promotion at work, the death of a dog, a child's achievement at school or the gulf that exists between themselves and their neighbours. When they do take place, these opening conversations can function in a number of ways. First, they can invite a re-evaluation of dominant assumptions about power relations between researchers and participants, throwing into question the idea that structural positioning – which often places the researcher in a position of power in relation to participants – translates straightforwardly into the micro-level interactions between individuals in the research setting (Mahony, 2018). They can also reveal a plethora of difficulties in a person's life, which in turn teaches us something about multiple disadvantage and the way that singular setbacks and life events can have cumulative effects, bouncing off each other, reproducing and re-entrenching hardships across different domains of life. Sometimes, these opening conversations reveal something that seems at first glance to have nothing whatsoever to do with our research, but which later transpires to be a fundamental part of the story – in this case a psychological process intended to distance the self from the stigma that has come to define being in debt.

Sally spends the next 90 minutes talking, slipping between the kitchen and the bottom of the stairs to shout up to the children as they descend further and further into discord, and to plead with them to end their incessant bickering. For the most part she seems at pains to distinguish herself from the imaginary others – the immorally indebted – emphasising how *her* story of problem debt is different from theirs.

She and her ex-husband Tony met at school when they were aged 14 and 16 respectively. They fell in love – "one of those whirlwind romances" – and by their early twenties they were married. She worked as an administrative assistant in a local school and Tony worked as a landscape gardener for a company contracted by the local authority to maintain the parks in the area. They saved enough money for a small deposit on a house – "with no help from anyone" – and in their mid-twenties took out a "hefty" mortgage and bought a three-bedroomed property near the school where Sally worked. They had used all their savings as a down payment for their home so they took out a loan for £4,000 to buy a car. Shortly afterwards they took out another loan, of £5,000, to do some work on the house – "nothing extravagant, necessary work, to make it homely, you know", then got a credit card and spent £6,000 on it taking Tony's parents on holiday for their silver wedding anniversary. In many ways they had arrived at the kind of life they had longed for, even if it was on borrowed funds.

Sally fell pregnant in her late 20s and had Caitlyn, then Damian, who she admits she "spoiled rotten" because she had grown up with an absent father, an itinerant mother and little in the way of material comfort. "I just wanted the best for my kids, I wanted them to have what I didn't have," she says. Sally gave up work to look after the children and the home, and things became tighter financially, but they scraped by each month on Tony's earnings and tax credits, paying all their outgoings and the loan repayments, but occasionally turning to her in-laws to meet their financial commitments when things got really tight. They took out a loan to buy a new car as their previous one was now too small and had seen better days.

Then Tony lost his job. The local authority gave the parks maintenance contract to another company, and the £1,600 he had brought home each month disappeared. Sally looked for work but found nothing that would fit around her childcare duties, which was her priority, and they relied for a while on Tony's redundancy money and £500 in Child Tax Credits. But that arrangement did not last long, and eventually Tony applied for out-of-work benefits. Sally says: "I mean we never wanted to sign on, I'm not like that, but just with the kids so young and that I didn't want to go out to work and dump them in a nursery." And she talks briefly about the people in her neighbourhood, how they don't even *try* to find work, but are happy signing on every week.

Over the next few months, with a reduced household income of around £1,000 in benefits, Sally and Tony defaulted on their mortgage repayments, which were around £600 a month, and Sally points out that they "tried hard to sort everything out", but putting food on the table and seeing the children warm, dry and well clothed were her overriding concerns. Cracks began to appear in their marriage, as they argued over what to do about their finances and tried to shield Caitlyn and Damian from the impact of their struggles. After a year of trying to make things work, Sally and Tony went their separate ways. They sold the house but came away with nothing in way of equity once they had paid the fees entailed in the sale, the arrears on the mortgage and most of the outstanding loans from their early married life.

Sally and the children moved into a rented flat, which was damp and cold, where they stayed for a few months until something better became available. Although most of the loans were cleared, by the time they moved to their current place Sally was really struggling; this was the first time she had managed her finances by herself. She received around £1,400 a month through Income Support, Tax Credits, Child Benefit and Housing Benefit, but Tony's child maintenance contributions were sporadic, and the money coming in did not allow Sally to cover the car loan repayments or the cost of living for her and the children, which amounted to around £1,600 a month. Sally started using her credit card for everyday expenses and at one point the outstanding balance reached £9,000. She missed a couple of months' repayments and fell behind with a bill for the Sky package and the gas and electricity. She started juggling her debts. Realising that the situation was not sustainable, she contacted her local branch of Citizens Advice, where she received support with how to get back on track. The choice she felt she faced was stark: live on her current income and fail to look after her children properly, find work and miss out on her children growing up, or live in the red. She is currently looking for work.

At one stage, Sally was getting three or four phone calls a day from the people she owed money to. "I kept telling them: 'I'm not long divorced, we lost our home, I'm not trying to screw you around. I'm not sitting here with cans of drink or out with the girls, I know where my priorities are and that's my home, my children and pay my bills, pay my way'." However, Sally says that events seemed to have conspired against her actually doing that. Talking directly to me she goes on: "I mean there's people with these massive debts and they're still smoking two packs of fags a day and using their benefits to pay for the like the top Sky packages and that, instead of just paying back the money they owe."

I ask Sally who she knows who does these things, and by way of an answer she points out of the kitchen window, taking in the whole estate and dismissing it with a flick of her wrist. She points out that she *only* smokes when she goes out for the *occasional* drink with friends, and that she just has a *basic* Sky package, not the most expensive one, and anyway she *needs* it for the children.

> 'And my car, I mean I've had people say to me "you can't be struggling, you've got a nice car" and I went "actually I do struggle and I need my car" ... And with my health problems and all that, I have that many appointments, then I've got the kids, in case anything happened with them, I *need* a car.'

I cannot help myself; I tell Sally that, to be honest, in all the interviews we have done for our debt research we have yet to meet these people, these other families living with problem debt who sit around determined not to work, smoking and drinking to excess, watching endless Sky movies and rubbing their hands together in glee at how they are getting one over on their creditors. And that, despite appearances, other people's circumstances seem to be much like hers, in their broadest terms: a low income, some pre-existing debt, an 'income shock' or two (or three, or more), followed by a spiral downwards into unsustainable financial hardship and desperate choices whose ripple effects are felt in every social relationship and in people's deepest sense of themselves. Perhaps they too have experienced similar challenges, hardships or traumas, can also justify their cars, and only smoke and drink occasionally as well, just to take the edge off every now and then? But Sally Other is not having it: "Oh no, there's loads of them round here, I can show you where they live if you want."

The interview with Caitlyn and Damian reveals very little in the way of knowledge about debt or money problems – it seems that Sally is doing a pretty good job of keeping up appearances in relation to them. But when asked about his neighbourhood, Damian mutters something under his breath and collapses in a fit of giggles, leaving it to Caitlyn to explain (in a fake American accent that has been growing more and more pronounced through the course of the interview) that "it's full of pikeys around here". The process of othering appears to have found its way into the suite of psychological tools at their disposal too.

Our time is up. Sally calls me a cab and issues a warning to keep my belongings zipped away out of sight, even in the taxi. While this signifies genuine concern on her part, it also seems to be her way of having the last word in differentiating herself from the others.

Sally is an expert in the art of othering; a peddler of a discourse that, through its setting up of binary subject positions, distinguishes her – the morally indebted – from her imagined, immoral counterparts. And it is easy to see how she has come to be so – stripped of the material assets needed to obtain or maintain a respected socioeconomic position in contemporary society, her identity work takes on a particular significance, as one of the few resources left to her to draw on in claiming a legitimate place in the world. For Sally, the process of othering is a survival tactic.

But in this are the seeds of self-destruction. For all her intention to reject the negative image of the immorally indebted, for all her hard work in maintaining a psychological distinction between her justifiable financial behaviour and the morally flawed decisions of others, she helps to keep the divisive discourse and its available subject positions alive, at once validating its claim to truth and sustaining it through circulation. And in doing this, she not only succeeds in sharpening a discursive tool with which she herself can cast doubt onto others' moral positioning and thereby boost her own, but she also – unwittingly, ironically – makes that tool available for others in turn to use against her. And as Patrick (2017, p 170) notes in her book *For whose benefit?*, othering 'operates to divide a potential "us" into multiple "others" … and thus undermines the possibility for a more solidaristic and progressive challenge to the status quo'.

There is no clear policy or set of policies through which to address the process of othering or the stigmatisation that gives rise to it. Like the corresponding *striver versus skiver* dichotomy within wider debates on poverty, work and welfare – brought to critical attention through the work of scholars such as Lister (2013), Jensen (2014) and Patrick (2017) – it is both more deep-rooted and more nebulous than any one specific policy recommendation might allow for. But addressing socioeconomic injustice is not only achieved through making specific amendments to existing policies, or by making more radical changes to the policy landscape. As explicitly recognised by Scott Paul (2016) in a Joseph Rowntree Foundation blog, bringing about progressive social change is also achieved through addressing the 'cultural values and deep frames' that underpin policies, funding decisions and wider public attitudes. As they stand, the values and deep frames in our society entail the conceptualisation of poverty as an individual rather than structural issue, and they stigmatise families struggling with debt as feckless and greedy, providing a culture of legitimacy for approaches that punish rather than support those – others – who have fallen into the debt trap.

NINE

Keeping up appearances

Sorcha Mahony

The taxi drives out of the city, through the suburbs and deep into a sprawling estate that has a cluster of high-rise flats in the middle, which tower over the grey concrete houses below. In places you cannot tell where the roofs end and the sky begins as the clouds swell and gather on the horizon. At Sandra's block I buzz the 'concierge' button and a Jamaican Geordie opens the door, smiling to reveal half a dozen gold teeth and explaining that Sandra has been called to a meeting at her son's school but will be back soon. He phones one of her neighbours and Barbara, a nervous, twitchy woman in her fifties, comes down to collect me and take me to wait at her flat. She leads the way through a concrete stairwell that smells of fresh paint and urine, up the stairs, out onto an exposed walkway and into her smoke-filled flat, where two young women are sitting on the sofa with their coats on. Barbara introduces me – "she's come all the way from London just to talk to Sandra about her leccy"– and they joke about how they would all like a personal visit from their electricity providers so that they could ask for a discount, and they talk about the upcoming community Santa parade that helps to take the edge off the winter.

For the next few minutes, the front door opens and shuts, opens and shuts, as people drift in and out of the flat and Barbara explains that half the block has keys – it is like a second home to them, they share everything. Then Sandra comes in, beaming and bouncy, and Barbara hands me over. We hurry across to Sandra's flat, her son Bailey leading the way on his bike, Sandra and I talking about the cold and the clouds, Sandra checking that I did not tell any of her neighbours why I am really there.

As soon as we are through the front door, Sandra ushers Bailey into the living room where his older sister is playing on the iPad, and tells them both to stay there until we have finished. Despite my request to invite her children for interviews, and despite my reassurances that I would not reveal anything to them about the debts or financial situation at home, Sandra had remained steadfast in her refusal to let me speak with them. So we go into the kitchen, she shuts the door behind her and we sit at the table, blowing warm air into our hands in a futile attempt to warm ourselves up.

In many ways, Sandra is a dream to interview, answering most of the questions on the schedule without them being asked and making the conversation seem natural and effortless. But there is an urgency in her voice. For the most part she rushes through her story, tripping over her words, interrupted only when the last of the natural light fades and she has to get up to find some matches in the drawer so she can light a candle, which she places on the table between us.

Until a year ago, Sandra worked as an office manager for a manufacturing company, a job she loved because the people there were like a second family to her. Her husband was employed as a painter and decorator but stopped 18 months previously when he was diagnosed with a chronic heart condition and told by his doctor not to work. For the first six months he was off, Sandra continued in her job, but got a call one day from her daughter, who had come home to find her father at the bottom of the stairs, his left leg broken in two places. Sandra tried juggling work and caring for her husband, but found it impossible to do both. She took some annual leave "to try and get him set up at home" but during that time came to understand the true extent of her husband's needs: how close he was teetering on the edge of depression, how isolated he had become from friends, how difficult he found it to manage the pain he experienced, and how easily he doubted his value as a husband and father. With a heavy heart, Sandra handed her notice in and became a full-time carer.

Even before her husband's diagnosis, life had not been plain sailing. Her daughter, now aged 19, was bullied so badly and for so long that she had stopped attending school and left before sitting her A Levels. The day she came home with her shirt ripped and a clump of her hair in her pocket, Sandra had marched up to the school and demanded to see the head teacher, but the bullying had continued – outside school and online – until her daughter stopped attending, closed her social media accounts and resigned herself to working in the local supermarket until she could apply for sixth-form college and start over. Sandra was so angry that she fantasised about finding the girls responsible and meting out some justice of her own. But she did not, and the anger ate away at her until it took over and she became a tense, prickly version of herself. Previous to this, Sandra's son, now aged 16, had been diagnosed with attention deficit hyperactivity disorder (ADHD) and autism spectrum disorder (ASD), a process that took years and enmeshed Sandra in a protracted battle with his school to get him the support he needed. His conditions were diagnosed as mild but he was increasingly prone to violent outbursts and particularly sensitive to changes in mood or circumstance around him, which meant that Sandra would often find him in his bedroom banging his head on the bedframe or pinching his legs until they bled, and she worried about him constantly, the bruises on his forehead looming in her mind's eye as she lay in bed in the early hours, unable to sleep.

So when her husband first fell ill and later broke his leg, these events were straws on the back of a camel already buckling under pressure, and Sandra's immediate priority was to try to restore some stability at home – to see that her husband was looked after, that her children were not suffering and that the relationships between each of them improved, or at least stopped deteriorating at the rate they had begun to. She approached her GP and joined a 20-month waiting list for family therapy.

Sandra knew there was a problem with money in the family. Although the household had started receiving a number of out-of-work benefits – Employment and Support Allowance and Disability Living Allowance for her husband, Disability Living Allowance for her son, Income Support and Carer's Allowance for herself and Housing Benefit for the family as a whole – the income was not as high as it had been when they were a working household, and anyway her husband's heart condition and recent disability were costly, what with travelling to all the appointments, increased insurance, money spent trying to cheer the family up and the alterations she had made to the house and car out of her own pocket. Sandra cannot remember the exact difference in amounts, she just knows that when they stopped working, things got much tighter financially. Initially she checked her bank balance obsessively and fretted when she did not have enough money to cover some small expense but after a while she stopped checking, just tried her luck at the cash machine and withdrew the money if it was there. She thought long and hard about what they could live without, but that only resulted in cancelling a long-forgotten gym membership, which did not make much of a difference to her monthly budget anyway. With meagre savings to fall back on, the treading water did not last long. Reminder notices started arriving for the water, rent, gas and electricity, for the service charges on the flat, for the hire purchase on the car, for the internet, telephone and television. These were followed by final notices, then letters from debt collection agencies demanding payment. She did not have the money to pay them all and so she paid some – she cannot remember which – and fell further behind with others. By now her husband had fallen into a full-blown depression, and Sandra spent the spare time she did not really have trying to support him, or attending ADHD and ASD training courses and appointments with her son. She got a £30 fine for the time she had taken her husband to hospital and, worrying that he would miss his appointment, forgot to buy a parking ticket. But she could not pay the fine and received a court order, which she put back in the envelope and returned to sender. She stopped opening the post and disconnected the doorbell.

Months passed and Sandra could not get back on track with the arrears on the household bills, so she got another credit card with a view to paying off all the outstanding balances and starting again with a clean slate. But she now had a credit card debt of over £8,000 and could not see any way of paying it off. She says that the benefits she had coming in just did not cover the cost of living for her family (although she is rather elusive at first when pressed on the details of her income and outgoings).

Until 2010, state benefits used to increase in line with the Retail Price Index (a process known as 'uprating'), such that the amount of support that eligible families received took account of rises in the cost of living. In 2010, the government delinked many benefit increases from the Retail Price Index, linking them instead to the Consumer Price Index, a change that resulted in many forms of welfare increasing below the rate of inflation. Then, in 2012, the government announced a 1% cap on increases to most key benefits, irrespective of continued rises in living costs, and this cap remained in place until 2015. In 2015, as part of its Welfare Reform and Work Act, the government announced a four-year benefits freeze, set to start the following year and run until 2020, meaning that many benefits would see no increase at all during this period, despite continuing – and higher-than-expected – inflation rates (see Royston, 2017). The anti-poverty lobby in the UK, comprising charities, think-tanks and academics, came out in force to dispute the freeze, and at the time The Children's Society warned that over seven million children living in over four million low-income households would be adversely affected (The Children's Society, 2016b). In the lead-up to the 2017 Budget announcement, the disquiet once again hit the headlines as many urged the government to scrap the freeze (see, for example, Buchan, 2017).

Sandra's benefits did not cover the cost of living for her and her family, and they were the lucky ones. Being in receipt of Disability Living Allowance meant that they were exempt from the benefits cap and freeze, that they were not subject to the same reduction in real terms as the millions of other families struggling to get by on dwindling state support. Still, the household income was insufficient at a time in Sandra's life when she and her family needed it more than ever.

I ask her how everyone copes. "*Everyone* doesn't cope, *I* do," she replies, her breath hanging in the air above the flickering candle light. "They haven't got a clue about any of this." She says that her priority is to protect her family from the financial turmoil around them, so she pretends that everything is fine. When her husband commented that he could not get out to the pub to watch Sky Sports, Sandra signed up for the top Sky subscription, and pays each month for a package she can ill afford, but which keeps him occupied and, she believes, from giving up altogether. When her son said that he wanted driving lessons, Sandra booked a block of them for his 17th birthday, and again the credit card debt crept up. Why should her son be punished and miss out on the same gift she had given her daughter for *her* 17th, and on something that had become a young person's ticket to adulthood? She continued to shop for brand-name groceries and clothes, lest her family should start to question why they were "living like paupers".

It is not unusual for parents to cry during these debt interviews; we ask about financial situations that have caused them distress, and these inevitably touch on traumatic life events – 'exogenous income shocks' – and more broadly on the question of parental competence. The tipping point for Sandra comes when she talks about a visit from her energy supply company, and once she starts crying she finds it hard to stop; every time she opens her mouth to speak about the visit, nothing comes out, so she closes it again and purses her lips together. She tries over and over and each time her eyes well up a little bit more until her tears are dropping onto the table and she is sitting with her hands over her face, sobbing quietly. "Sorry, I just needed to get that out," she says after a while, sniffing and sweeping the hair from her cheeks. "They just made me feel so small. Waving these official-looking papers around in my face. I was mortified. I felt so, so small."

Staff from the energy company had installed prepayment meters outside Sandra's flat to recoup the debt that had remounted on the accounts, but even then Sandra had continued to hide what was going on from the people around her. Neighbours had gathered, she had panicked as she struggled to think up a plausible explanation for what was happening, and in the end told everyone that she had asked for the meters so that she could keep a closer eye on how much energy they were using.

Feelings of guilt started to gnaw away at Sandra's sense of self. Not only was she unable to sort this financial mess out, and not only was she concealing the truth to the people she loved most in the world, but she was also now lying outright to everyone. "I know it's stupid," she says, "but I don't want people I know judging me. I don't want my kids thinking I'm a bad mum. A parent should be able to provide for their kids."

Sandra has told one person about her debts and the wider financial precariousness that has allowed them to spiral: the concierge I met down in the lobby. "He's a good mate, he is, I know he won't tell anyone and he doesn't judge me, he just listens. I don't know what I'd do without him." No friend, no neighbour, no ex-colleague, no support service, nobody else knows what she is going through, not even her partner. Recent research by Relate, the relationship counselling service, reveals that Sandra is not alone: 47% of their survey respondents who had household debts, had not told their partner about them (Relate, 2017).

"I'm like a duck, me," Sandra announces. "People see me bobbing about all chirpy and quacky and that, but underneath my feet are paddling like crazy to stop me from drowning." And sometimes this works, to a degree: her children have not had to go without, despite insufficient funds. But it is expensive, and it means that the pressure piles up on Sandra. She is exhausted and stressed and it does not take a lot to push her under – a vase accidentally knocked over, a cup of tea spilled and not cleaned up properly, someone leaving the lid off the toothpaste. "And that's not a pretty sight. The kids'll be like 'uh-oh mum's losing it again' and they just stay out the way for a couple of days."

We wrap up Sandra's interview and on the way out she points to a dent in the kitchen door where she punched it in a rage when her sister refused to lend her money because Sandra would not tell her what it was for, as she could not bear to admit to being unable to "pay for the basics". "That really freaked the kids out that did. I felt so bad. Bailey, he had the look of fear in his eyes."

By the end of Sandra's interview it is clear why there are no children and no partner to speak with in her household – her compulsion to keep up appearances is so strong. It is also clear why the interview was a somewhat hurried affair and why Sandra bundles me surreptitiously out of the door and down the stairs to wait for a cab when it finishes.

In the lobby the concierge talks about his job, explaining that his role is part caretaker, part building rep, part social worker, part welfare officer, part counsellor and part friend. He also whispers that, unbeknown to any of the residents, he has recently been informed that cuts to local government mean that his position is being disbanded in a few months' time and the crucial function he delivers will soon cease to exist. "What will happen after that?" I ask, thinking of Sandra and how he is her only confidant and support. "I'll look for another job and they'll be on their own," he replies, rubbing the stubble on his chin and shaking his head.

Outside it is dark and it has started to hail, the little round stones bouncing off the ground and lashing down on the car windscreens, their wipers swishing and bumping furiously. Families scuttle for shelter wherever they can find it, and a couple comes tumbling into the lobby with their toddler in a pushchair, bags of nappies hanging off the handles and shopping spilling out of their arms. The concierge runs around from behind the counter to help them and there is something both reassuring and sad in his efforts: they evoke such a sense of refuge and domesticity, but any semblance of sanctuary now seems so illusory, just a matter of appearances.

TEN

The child

Sorcha Mahony

Bianca Bottello has come unstuck from her age.[4] She floats around in the hinterlands of poverty and debt, a child according to national and international convention, a teenager – just – but not able to afford to live like one, and undertaking many of the tasks and financial responsibilities thought to be the preserve of adulthood. She attends school and plays childhood games with friends during the week, reads teenage magazines at the weekends and through this skirts the edges of youth culture and identity, and every day plays a crucial role in navigating the rocky terrain of financial struggle at home.

We sit on the edge of her mother and father's bed, which is strewn with laundry, magazines, paperwork and toiletries, clothes spilling out of the chest of drawers that is jammed up against the bedframe, old toys stuffed into the cupboard that is balanced on top of it, and Bianca tells me about her family, about their problems with money, and about the part she has played in trying to sort things out.

Bianca is 13 years old. She lives with her mother, father and older brother in a tiny three-bedroomed maisonette in the north-west of England. Her father works in the building trade, she and her older brother go to school, and her mother no longer works, having lost her job as a youth worker about a year previously. While Bianca may not have an overview of the household finances, she understands that they are not rich and that the money coming in does not always stretch far enough. Although she feels comfortable, cared for and loved, she has gone without in the past, and understands the contexts that have made this necessary. She is actively involved in the household budgeting:

'Mum's always got bills to pay so like it's hard. At Christmas me and her like sat there and planned what food we're going to buy and she was like "I need to put £100 aside for the gas and electric bill" and then we planned the rest of it out from that. We cut back on a lot of stuff, like a lot of luxuries, like we didn't go out at all, like we didn't go on holiday and things like that, because we just couldn't afford it, so.'

Bianca feels proud of helping her mother cope financially, but it sounds as though her mother struggles to accept her daughter's support. Bianca says:

'My mum apologises for when I help. She goes "sorry I know you're not supposed to do this at your age" and that sort of hurts me because I'm there to help her and she's apologised for something that I just do because I want to do it for my mum and it hurts…. It burns me inside when my mum cries. It's hard for me to see that … I love her no matter what. I'd turn this house upside down for her. It's like my choice to help. She's my mum. I love her no matter what. She's like, she's just my best friend.'

And in the way she articulates the emotional strain, the depth of her love and the strong sense of capability she feels, Bianca seems beyond her years.

While her peers are preoccupied with acquiring the trappings of contemporary youth culture, Bianca focuses her attention on saving all the money she can for the important things in life. I wonder aloud what she thinks the important things in life are, and she says:

'Well like, loads of, my, like, friends have got iPhones and that and everything and like I don't have one of them. I chose that decision by myself that I wouldn't be, like, I wouldn't spend my money on sweets and stuff. I wouldn't spend it on, like, anything that doesn't matter in life. Like I would first, I would get like money for university. That would be my first decision that I would make, and then the money what I'd get left over, I'll probably save it until I was old enough to buy a house and to get a car and to know that I have, like, some money that I can actually do that and know that I've saved enough money for what I can do in my future.'

As well as saving for her future and helping with the household budget, Bianca has supported her mother in sorting out some of the debts, accrued in light of the general reduction in household income following her mother's redundancy, and in particular in the wake of an unexpectedly high energy bill:

'I remember like, last winter when we had the heating on and we had them on and it was like really cold but I remember like, when she got the bill afterwards and it was like mum was really stressed out about it. So she was talking to me about, like how much she was going to have to pay and stuff because I think it was over a thousand pounds, the bill was. And she only put £100 aside. So that was like really hard, straight after Christmas. And I was trying to help her out with how she was supposed to sort it out so that she'd got enough money to pay everything, like trying to kind of sort it all out. She was like, worrying about it, so, I don't like it when she gets stressed out obviously. I was like worried for her because, well like it was pretty scary to be honest.'

Bianca and her family are one of many struggling with their fuel bill. The price of energy has been the subject of intense debate – and disquiet – in the UK since at least 2013, when murmurings of a political price intervention first arose, as customers were paying increasingly high costs for the fuel that kept their homes liveable and their families warm and dry. While different kinds of government support have been made available for certain vulnerable customers – for example in the form of the Warm Home Discount Scheme, the Cold Weather Payment, the Winter Fuel Payment and the Prepayment Meter Cap – there is widespread acknowledgement that the energy market does not work fairly or in the interest of consumers, especially those living on low incomes or experiencing other disadvantages in their lives (see, for example, Rayner et al, 2017). Related to this, there has been growing awareness of fuel poverty over the years, and of the effects this can have on families, with charities such as National Energy Action working tirelessly to support the estimated four million fuel-poor households in the UK, and with The Children's Society drawing special attention to the effects that fuel poverty can have on children (The Children's Society and National Energy Action, 2015).

The lack of competition in the energy market came under particular scrutiny after Ofgem – the energy industry regulator – published a review in March 2014, conducted with the Office of Fair Trading, in which it reported on a significant degree of uncertainty and distrust among consumers, alongside rising profits for the so-called 'Big Six' energy giants (Ofgem, 2014). Following this initial review, Ofgem referred the retail energy market for full investigation by the Competition and Markets Authority (CMA) – the industry watchdog – which reported in June 2016 on a number of 'remedies' along with a suggested implementation strategy, but which fell short of recommending an energy price cap (CMA, 2016).

In the spring of 2017, prior to the snap General Election, the Prime Minister, Theresa May, committed to capping energy prices in order to help the estimated 17 million households subject to 'unfair' price hikes on standard variable tariffs. By the time of the Conservative Party conference in the autumn of that year, May had resurrected her pledge to fix the 'broken energy market' and published draft legislation to cap excessive prices (Department for Business, Energy and Industrial Strategy, 2017).

As the draft Domestic Gas and Electricity Bill makes its way through Parliament, as Ofgem and the government wrangle over where the responsibility lies in tackling the issue of 'rip-off' energy costs (see, for example, Vaughan, 2017) and as some energy companies lambast the proposed cap for being 'crude' and stifling competition (see Ambrose, 2017), it continues to fall to children like Bianca Bottello to help her family deal with their debts on the energy bills they cannot afford.

Bianca talks about the various ways she helped her mother cope with the fallout from the fuel bill the previous winter. She says:

> '[Mum] doesn't really like to ask for help 'cos she doesn't, she gets embarrassed. When the bill came I had to like force her to ask family for help because, you know when like there was no money and generally, we were running out of food and I was like "you need to ask nan, you *need* to ask them to lend you some money until next week". Like, even like, sometimes I lend her some money from my jar but she hates taking that. She doesn't like to ask, she likes to do it on her own but sometimes you just can't, so.'

Bianca is not alone in her efforts to support her family through financial hardship and problem debt. While many of the parents in our debt research go to great lengths to hide their financial struggles from their children, shouldering the burden alone to try to protect them (to greater or lesser degrees of success), not all can and not all choose to. Some children are not only aware of the predicaments that their parents are in, but are also actively involved in managing the family's money troubles. They give cash, acquired through extended family, birthdays, Christmases, and visits from the tooth fairy for the younger ones. They answer the door and the telephone to creditors and in the process become gatekeepers, shielding the family from demands they cannot meet. They devise tactics for interest-free borrowing, playing key roles in tapping into wider networks and the resources within them. They cut back on their consumption levels in a drive to free up parental income for paying bills. They curb their desires for the things and experiences their friends have, and sometimes they tell themselves that this is good. Those whose parents do not read English translate financial documents such as bills and reminder notices for money owed. Whatever the nature of their contributions, children and young people are sometimes deeply involved in managing the fallout from poverty and debt, in shaping their family's coping tactics, in fashioning what we might think of as a new 'weapon of the weak' (Scott, 1985). And they often undertake these tasks with a strong sense of moral autonomy, doing them because they are necessary but emphasising their choice and gaining a felt moral edge over their peers in the process. They display a sense of pride and intrinsic worth that no amount of material goods can compete with.

And in these endeavours, young people remind us that when they live, consciously, with significant financial instability, it is easy to become decoupled from their chronological stage of life – children but with an understanding and articulation beyond their years, teenagers but not 'youth' in the sense of enjoying all that this has come to mean in terms of consumption and related identity positions, adults in some of the responsibilities they shoulder, yet enjoying none of the privileges ostensibly associated with adulthood.

Anthropologists and historians have long recognised 'how diverse and elastic a concept childhood can be' (Montgomery, 2009, p 3), that while childhood is characterised by a state of physical immaturity the world over, it is a social construct that has been invented – as historians such as Cunningham (2006) and Aries (1962) before him have convincingly argued – and the particular form it takes varies significantly from culture to culture and over time. But despite this recognition, a strong normative discourse persists that posits childhood as a 'precious time ... a separated and safe space' (UNICEF, 2005, unpaginated), and when children's lives deviate from this ideal-type in an obvious manner, we have ways of making sense of this: When we look to children in the developing world who play central roles in the productive labour market and in the daily struggle to survive in a context of absolute and chronic poverty, we might invoke the notion of cultural relativity but remain moved, labelling them as 'child labourers' and asking ourselves what we can do to help. When children in the UK care for family members who have physical or mental health problems or misuse drugs or alcohol, we conceptualise them as 'young carers' and support them accordingly.

But for young people like Bianca Bottello, stuck in the backwaters of financial insecurity, neither young carers (but caring deeply and manifesting this in various ways), nor exploited child labourers (but working hard to help keep their families afloat), it is not clear how we can best understand them. There seems to be no category capable of galvanising increased consideration for their predicaments, no label that might command more nuanced attention from policy makers, no clear way of naming the extent of their contributions without undermining their autonomy. There is certainly no straightforward means of capturing the way that the socioeconomic structures that constrain them also enable them, offering up spaces for fulfilling a deep-felt sense of filial obligation and making available subjectivities they are proud of. They are just poor, in relative terms, and indebted – the children of families who struggle to get by and repay what they owe, contributing in ways that make us question whether the categories we have for understanding them are really up to the job.

There are no longer any outstanding bills in Bianca's household. Due in part to the role she has played at home, her family are financially solvent, if still materially disadvantaged. At the end of our interview I hand Bianca a 'signposting and complaints' leaflet, given to all of our participants, with details of who to contact if she wants to complain about the research process, which includes the Childline telephone number in case our discussion has caused her any distress. She furrows her brow. "Isn't that for kids who are like abused and that?", she asks, unimpressed with the implications of the leaflet, possibly questioning whether what she has been trying to tell me has been understood at all. "It's like I said, I do that stuff 'cos I want to do it; no one's forcing me, it's like my choice." And I leave knowing that I still do not fully understand what it is like to come unstuck from your age in this way, and to gain such a lot in the process.

ELEVEN

The tyranny of the small things

Sorcha Mahony

"Get the door will you, Tom?", a woman's voice calls out, and an upstairs window is pushed open with the end of a crutch. "He'll be with you in a minute, pet," the voice calls down before the window closes, and I wait on a rickety wooden bench in the front yard. Tom, a tall, slender boy in his late teens, opens the front door and his mother hobbles downstairs behind him, her right leg in plaster up to the knee. With no room for introductions in the narrow hall, Tom leads the way through the kitchen and into the dining area.

"Sorry, we're decorating, it's a bit of a mess," Tom's mother says, and I think of all the other homes I've visited for our debt research, similarly suspended mid-refurb, and I wonder what it might mean – the abandonment of a dream? Hope of a fresh start? Life on hold?

"Kids, in here," Tom's mother calls, and children seem to spill out of the adjoining living room. "This is Tom, he's 17, Mikey, 14, Leah, nine and Darrell, six, they're mine, and these lot live next door, don't yous? I'm just watching them for a bit. Oh and I'm Helen." She pats each of the children on the head as she introduces them, and the younger ones laugh, lighting up the room with their toothless grins. "You can go there," Helen nods towards the dining table, and Tom and I sit down as Helen and the children pile back into the living room, the theme tune to the animated television series *SpongeBob SquarePants* almost drowning out the squabbles over who sits where.

We tread carefully at first, talking about how Tom spends his time, about his role as big brother, about how his mother broke her ankle, but it does not take long before we wander into financial territory and it becomes apparent that, while Tom does not know the finer-grained detail of his mother's income, outgoings or debts, he knows about their money problems and debts in general – and that his mother owes thousands – and about the effects of this on him and the rest of the family.

Ever since Tom can remember, the situation at home has oscillated between manageable and hard. From the age of six, he was aware of not having as much as his friends at school – of his jumper being scruffier than others', of not being able to join in conversations about holidays abroad. He says: "We've never been like, I don't know, like wealthy … the whole of my life really it's just sort of been like, up and down." But things started to get much worse a few years previously, around the time his father left. His mother used to have three part-time jobs, working as a playground supervisor in a school, a domestic cleaner and a childminder, but she stopped the childminding and the cleaning to be around for the children more after their father moved out, so suddenly the household income was squeezed even tighter. His mother does not get paid a lot, owes people money and is always fretting about how to pay it back, and his father's contributions barely cover the cost of feeding them for a few days. He muses that, while his friends take 'money problems' to mean not having enough to go out and get drunk at the weekend, for Tom "it's about household stuff … about getting food in and bills paid and paying people back what we owe them".

"We've had to just sort of, you know, not spend as much on food really. We've had to cut back a lot and mum's just been very down … but we try to get by as best we can." Tom talks about clothes, about really wanting to replace his ripped jeans and his trainers with the soles that are flapping off, but not being able to afford to because the money that comes in gets spent on 'essentials' or repaying money owed. And he describes the way poverty stands between him and his friends, an invisible wall that separates them, growing taller by the day and mocking the bonds of friendship:

'I find, like, I don't know, say they go out on the wig [out drinking], I can't go because I haven't got the money. Like, if they go to golf or the lido or just like sort of regular things, the cinema, anything, I haven't got the money to do it. And, you know, like they go on holidays and that's expensive, the prices keep going up and I can't afford it. So it sort of hinders my relationship with my friends, yes. I mean, they'd offer, like say "oh no, I'll pay for you" but I don't like that, it's not something I want to bring to a discussion, it's embarrassing, it's just kind of like something I keep to myself. So I usually don't end up going out with them. We've all grown up with each other since we were little as well, so it's quite sad, really, to see us sort of like drifting apart into our different little worlds.'

Being broke and in debt affects Tom's mood:

'You can just be really grumpy all the time and I mean my brother and sister and me are always arguing over money and that, like saying "well, why don't *you* help more" sort of thing, contribute to mum more. And, you know, it's all this back-and-forth nonsense. It changes the whole mood of the house…. It causes mood swings between all of us and then like, you know, we're all pissed off with each other … it's just like a stress. It's just so sad that money has to control everything you know? But that's the way it is.'

He goes on to say that they are in quite a bit of debt at the moment:

'I'm not sure what the word is that I'm looking for but we like to sort of just try to work things out ourselves between us before bringing other people into it or whatever. But sometimes we can't. We're struggling a lot right now. Because it's sort of one of those years where it's going really down again so we're just trying to build everything back up.'

And he talks about riding the "repetitive rollercoaster" of job hunting, and about how his 15-year-old sister is also looking for part-time work.

'I just hate it where I'm sort of standing around and not doing anything; I have to do something … I try to focus in on actually how to pay the bills…. Like, with mum's debts, I'll always tell her to tell me because whatever I can do to try and help, you know.'

Tom describes the efforts he has gone to, to try to find a job since he left school (early) two years previously: the agencies he has signed up with, the aptitude tests, the questions he answered incorrectly, the online applications, the stress of waiting, the rejections and the anger he directs inwards. But so far his endeavours have only resulted in a couple of short-term, temporary contracts.

With no earnings to provide for himself or his family and help repay the debts, and with secure work hovering on the distant horizon, Tom says he contributes financially by "just being careful with the small things". "What small things?" I ask, and he goes on to explain the rules governing household consumption, rules that seem to come from a different era, more fitting of a war-time rationing effort than the life of a teenager in contemporary Britain:

- one cup of tea each in the morning, sharing the tea bag between them;
- two slices of bread each for breakfast;
- no snacks between meals;
- one teaspoon of ketchup when they have chips for dinner;
- one squirt of shower gel each per day;
- shampoo once a week, no conditioner;

- two sheets of toilet roll per visit to the toilet (and only flush the toilet if it is a number two);
- no heat-producing electrical products, such as hairdryers or blow heaters.

"We don't say goodnight to each other when we go to bed, we ask: 'Have you switched everything off?'" They monitor themselves closely and police each other, coming down hard when somebody breaks the rules in an effort to free up money so that their mother can repay her debts, and it sounds like a miniature version of Bentham's Panopticon. I ask Tom what the future looks like, and he replies: "I just hope I can start bringing in more money for us. It's all I really want for the future."

So much of Tom's daily life is determined by this multitude of small directives, their combined effects bigger than the sum of their parts, weighing down on him until his world shrinks to comprise little but the daily grind of making do. It is a life of chronic denial in a world of plenty, where the repression of fundamental desires is the norm and the meeting of basic needs is not a given, despite a broader context defined by material prosperity. And in this it seems like a life half lived; a life under the tyranny of the small things. "But it's just normal for me," Tom remarks, "though it's sort of like everything you do you're so limited. It's like it's not a big deal, but it does get you down, it does kind of rule your life a bit, you know?"

He goes on:

'I can go into a very negative mindset where I start blaming myself…. There are times where I, you know, I feel very like, I have a lot of anxiety problems because I feel if I don't do something, you know, the whole household could start going down really bad and whatever. So I'm always sort of battling myself, constantly battling myself. I've always got the constant sort of feeling that I need to do this, I need to do that, but it's never enough.'

In the initial *Debt trap* publication (The Children's Society and StepChange Debt Charity, 2014), we reported that 58% of children surveyed in households with problem debt said that they were worried about their family's financial circumstances, and a quarter of parents in those households said that their debts and money problems left their children feeling anxious and stressed. In our follow-up research into the links between debt and money problems on the one hand, and children's mental health and wellbeing on the other, we found that children in households with problem debt 'are five times more likely to have low wellbeing than those with no difficulties with debt' (The Children's Society, 2016a, p 26). We also found that problem debts can have negative effects on children independent of low income and other, more general money worries, and that the combination of low income and debt is especially damaging (The Children's Society, 2016a, p 11). Our analysis of data from the fifth wave of the Millennium Cohort Study suggests that, for low-income households, the greater the number of debts (rather than the amount of debt itself), the greater risk to children's mental health (The Children's Society, 2016a, p 12).

I ask Tom about signposting and support – whether the family has received any in light of their debts and financial difficulties. And he says no. Not once in all the time they have experienced problem debts – and it has been years, on and off – have any of their creditors signposted them to a debt advice service or towards more general provision catering for people struggling psychologically with the fallout from financial hardship and debt. And here, again, Tom is not alone. There is currently no common approach among creditors or debt advice providers to enquiring about the mental health or wellbeing of people living in indebted households, and there is no shared approach to signposting towards services that provide support. Provision in these areas is patchy, due in part to the current lack of statutory guidance around creditor and debt advice behaviour. People like Tom might or might not be adequately supported or referred, and when they are not, it is easy to see how all of the small things, undertaken with a view to being debt free and to gaining a sense of capability, might become burdensome and leave a person feeling like a failure, like whatever they do it is not enough.

We wrap up Tom's interview with a discussion about the simple pleasures of doing the things that do not cost money – a walk in the park, being outside on a sunny day – and apparently buoyed up by the positive turn in the conversation, Tom smiles and says something about how environmentally friendly they must be, how we might save the planet if more people took their cue from the consumption habits that his family has adopted. Although the interview is supposed to end on an encouraging note, this does not mean romanticising hardship, and anyway it is hard to see beyond the life of frugality that Tom and his siblings are living, a life that is not of their choosing, that has no legitimised place in the broader socioeconomic or cultural landscape, that is characterised by a multitude of small money-saving tactics, which together function to stifle everyday living. "We'll be alright, we'll find a way through," Tom insists, but again it is difficult to see beyond his earlier description of his mother's low-paid, low-status work and his own fruitless search for permanent employment, made increasingly difficult by his dwindling confidence and mounting anxiety. But suddenly the children tumble out of the lounge, and the dining room is full of giggles and screams and bodies crawling under the table, compelling Tom to smile and seek them out with pincer-like hands. And I play along with the apparent optimism; maybe things will be alright for him after all, maybe there are enough little people in his life to counterbalance all the small things that have come to weigh so heavily on his mind.

TWELVE

Juggling

Larissa Pople

"We are a classic example of riches to rags," says Said affably, and I wonder how much sympathy I am going to have for this couple. Said is on his second marriage, and has a grown-up son and daughter from his first marriage, who went to private school. "It has been quite a fall from grace," he remarks wryly.

The fall, for Said and Maryam, turns out to be due to illness and a related loss of earnings. When he was in his mid-forties, Said developed an aggressive strand of multiple sclerosis and experienced an unusually rapid deterioration in mobility combined with a lot of pain. Within months, he had stopped working for the consultancy where he was a senior partner, and the family's financial landscape changed radically. Maryam had her own small business as an interior designer so Said helped her with the finances and took on a few consultancy projects that he could do from home with the occasional trip down to London for a meeting. But increasingly he found it difficult to sit or stand for long, and often needed to take strong painkillers, so he was limited in the type and amount of work that he could do. Before long, he stopped working altogether, and they became reliant on his disability benefit to top up Maryam's modest earnings from her design work.

Part of the problem for Said was that his illness not only led to a dramatic drop in the family's income, but also required them to make extensive modifications to their home. They own their home – an unremarkable semi-detached house on a cul-de-sac in an affluent suburb of the West Midlands – but as they had to revert the mortgage to interest-only, they are approaching the end of the mortgage term with no prospect of paying off what they owe. "I think we probably own about two tiles on this house," he says.

When he first became ill, Said was still paying child maintenance to his ex-wife for his two older children, so his depleted income needed to stretch to two families. The dramatic change in fortunes required considerable adjustment – both psychologically and logistically – and for a period of time, he buried his head in the sand. He extended the overdraft on his current account with little effort and once the maximum was reached, new bank accounts were opened for the sole purpose of making use of the overdraft facilities. Having crossed the line between the red and black many times before, often with substantial sums of money involved, multiple overdrafts felt acceptable, hardly like 'debts' at all. But in the past there had always been the prospect of money around the corner to settle what was owed, and he felt like an equal partner in these financial transactions.

A far cry, then, from a current reality in which deterioration defines every aspect of life, except the needs of his family that have to be met. After the overdrafts, Said found that credit cards were necessary "to pay for food or get cash out to pay the Council Tax". And once these were exhausted, it was onto payday loans. With a long, healthy credit history built up during the first 20 years of his working life, borrowing was all too easy for Said, especially if he could do so online, and avoid the embarrassment of admitting to a real-life person that he needed cash. "They'd do a quick check, and you'd have the money in your account within 10 minutes."

Maryam and Said make financial juggling look like an art form, which is no great surprise given that Said has been responsible for multi-million pound budgets in a professional capacity, and Maryam seems to have financial competence coursing through her veins. Still, the dexterity with which they juggle their financial affairs is impressive, and challenges the popular assumption that people living with problem debt are lacking in financial acumen.

It is Maryam who is in charge of their outgoings, and she does so with ingenuity and razor-sharp attention to detail. The family eats much less meat than they used to – which she tells the boys is for ethical reasons – but if someone needs a new pair of shoes, "mushrooms are on the menu every night". She scours charity shops and car-boot sales to acquire costly items for the boys such as bikes and scooters, and sells on anything valuable that is lying around.

'I think the only thing left is the family computer, and Ibrahim's tablet, which is looking very tempting at the moment. I'm looking at that thinking "that's the mortgage". But I won't do that because I remember my dad doing it to me as a kid, taking all my money....'

Said is in charge of the household income. His approach is to stay up late, poring over the cashflow in the hope that things might have miraculously improved since he last looked, and make applications for payday loans at two o'clock in the morning. The next day, realising that he has forgotten that half term is fast approaching and Maryam is hoping to take the boys to the cinema, or that new football boots are needed, it is back to late-night computing to apply for another loan. Often he is in the position of 'robbing Peter to pay Paul', the decision of the day being which financial transactions to prioritise. "It's like juggling plates with people throwing chainsaws in every so often."

One of the ironies in their story is that in some ways their financial competence has prolonged their pain by postponing the point at which support became available to them. For a lengthy period of time, careful budgeting – and increasing indebtedness – kept them 'afloat'. As long as they found ways to keep paying the minimum payments to creditors, the family was not considered in 'financial difficulty' and therefore entitled to help. They are also in the unfortunate situation of not being poor enough to be eligible for certain entitlements, but not wealthy enough to have savings to fall back on.

The fact that they own their own home means that, in theory, they have the option of selling up, clearing their debts and going into rented accommodation. But this would be difficult in the area where they live – it is just too expensive. And moving away is not an attractive prospect, as they would have to move the boys away from the schools where they are settled. Another consequence of owning their own home is that help with the mortgage is more limited and difficult to access than it would be if they were renting.

Said's view is that it is in nobody's interest that their family or others like them lose their homes and "join the queue for social housing". The current housing crisis has many features: soaring rents, rising homelessness and increasing recourse to temporary accommodation. A large and growing number of children live in temporary accommodation: in the second quarter of 2017, 77% of households in temporary accommodation had dependent children, and the numbers have been rising year on year (Department for Communities and Local Government, Homelessness Statistics, table 775). In parallel, there has been a steady rise in the proportion of homeless households with dependent children: in 1998/99, 59% of homeless households had dependent children, but by 2016/17 this had risen to 68% (Department for Communities and Local Government, Homelessness Statistics, table 773). Homelessness due to the end of an assured shorthold tenancy – now the most common explanation for homelessness – more than doubled from 15% in 1998/99 to 32% in 2016/17. Helping families like Said's to remain in their own homes must be part of the solution.

Maryam being self-employed is another hurdle. It means that she has to handle her own tax, and with her income fluctuating, their eligibility for tax credits – which are paid in advance – has been variable. On more than one occasion they have found themselves in a position of receiving money that they are not entitled to and having to pay it back.

Maryam and Said have made the conscious decision to shield their children as much as possible from knowledge about their financial circumstances, which has meant trying to keep up appearances to a certain degree. The boys are too young to remember how life was different when the money was flowing, and neither do they appreciate that their half-brother and half-sister have had a very different upbringing to them. They used to go to karate club at their local leisure centre, but nowadays they only go to activities that are run by the school, as these are subsidised. When a school friend is having a birthday party at Quasar, Maryam politely offers their excuses for not going.

Despite both having family who are relatively wealthy, Said and Maryam see no other option than to face up to their financial problems alone. Maryam tells me that she borrowed a couple of thousand pounds from her sister at one point, hastening to add that this is a loan on which they are paying interest. But even though her sister has offered to help further, Maryam is emphatic that she does not want to take on further debts.

Despite – or maybe even because of – their debt problems, they have never felt closer as a couple. Said admits that he had never appreciated the agility with which Maryam juggled her work and childcare responsibilities, so being at home was an eye-opener for him. An added consequence of Maryam taking on the role of main breadwinner was that he became closer to the children, with greater involvement in the everyday details of their lives.

Said says: "Our marriage has been through the mill but it's much stronger for it." I reflect on this statement long after Maryam and Said's interview, mostly going round in circles as to how it could be reflected in a report without undermining the overall message around the damaging effects of debt. In the end I determine that it probably can't, that it is one of those things that *I* will have to juggle with until I can find a suitable format for its expression.

THIRTEEN

The downside of help

Larissa Pople

"Well you 'elp out your family don't ya? That's just what you do." Tasha is what her east-end friends would call a 'grafter'. From inauspicious beginnings, she has hauled herself up the career ladder with unwavering determination. Her childhood memories are of her parents working long hours in the busy pub that they ran together. They were one of those families with friends in abundance and very little money in their pockets as they were always letting people off the few pence that they were short of a pint. One thing that was instilled firmly in Tasha's mind when she was growing up, though, was that "you never get anything in life unless you work hard". So work hard she did: at school, at college, to land herself "a proper job" at the council, and to work her way up into a middle-tier management position there. Earning a decent salary of £40,000 a year, which made it possible to bring up her own three children in relative comfort – a far cry from the financial hardship of her own childhood – she surpassed even her own expectations.

Yet, when the time came for Danny, the eldest of her three children, to consider his post-compulsory education options, Tasha's long-held belief in striving for self-betterment ended up being the catalyst for her financial undoing. It had always been her expectation that her children would go on to higher education, so when Danny decided that he wanted to study economics at university, Tasha supported him every step of the way. He was eligible for a maintenance grant, and took out a student loan, but these only went part way to covering the costs of living away from home, so he found himself a part-time bar job to supplement his income. When it became clear that this was a distraction from his studies, Tasha stepped in to top up the grant from her own pocket.

Using her overdraft facility and a credit card to pay for his weekly online shopping and a portion of his rent, she saw her outgoings increase substantially during his first year of university. Nonetheless, things felt just about under control. Then Paige – who is 18 months younger than Danny but only one academic year behind him – went off to study sport science at university a year later, and Tasha started to feel as if she was losing a grip on her finances. Two more credit cards were needed, followed by a loan to pay off the credit cards. Before long she was in arrears on her own utility bills. How had it come to this?

A few years earlier, around the time that her youngest daughter, Skye, was born, Tasha had bought her own home with the help of a shared ownership scheme. The flat was tiny, but it was *hers*: an unimaginatively shaped rectangle containing two small bedrooms and an open-plan kitchen/dining area that doubled as a lounge. Danny and Paige shared a bunk bed in one of the bedrooms, and Tasha and baby Skye slept in the other. For five of Danny and Paige's teenage years, the family enjoyed their own type of domestic bliss there, but by the time of our interview, the debt had taken its toll on their living arrangements.

Wiping tears from the corner of her eyes, Tasha explains that she and Skye had to move in with Derek – her on-off partner, and the children's father – a few months previously so that she could rent out her flat. Ultimately she can see no other option than to sell her home. She has recently had it valued with a view to putting it on the market in the coming weeks. It feels like a hugely retrograde step; like everything she has strived so hard for has come to nothing. It is not as if Derek is a 'bad apple', she is keen to point out, but his presence in their lives has always been unreliable, and she much prefers being answerable only to herself. Over the past two decades, he has contributed very little to the family's income. Yet now that she is weighed down with debts, he has all sorts of opinions on the matter, including what she should or should not be spending her money on.

"While I was living on my own I had a self-worth. I feel like I had my own freedom, and could go out with my friends. I have lost my freedom." Tasha has not bought herself any clothes for two years. All of the little things she used to enjoy – going out for a drink with friends, going to the gym or to a Zumba class after work – have had to stop. She even cancelled the contract on her mobile phone at one point, but this was a step too far for her children so Danny, who is now working, bought her a cheap pay-as-you-go phone and has been topping up the credit every week. She walks an hour to work every day because the cost of public transport is prohibitively high in her current circumstances. When her colleagues talk in their coffee breaks about their holiday plans, it is like a kick to the stomach. For as long as she can remember, she has been promising Skye that she will take her on holiday, but at the bottom of their hearts, they both know that this is fantasy.

At the age of 10, it is easy to imagine that Skye is blissfully ignorant of what is going on. But Tasha is under no illusion that this is the case. "With my little one, if I wanted to pay her for chores, she will say: 'But you don't need to pay me.'" Skye may not understand all the specifics of the household budget, but she is attuned to the financial stress that her mother is under through other details such as that "she's always making calls to the bank" and, as a result, she adjusts her demands accordingly.

> 'I try to resist if I want something. If I want something really bad then I'll ask my mum and if she says no then I'll be okay.... Like sometimes I want Lego toys but I can't really have them, and sometimes I want more clothes but I can't really have them either.'

There are some costs that are unavoidable: the cost of Skye's breakfast club and after-school clubs, the childminder, the school uniform. The burdens of being a working parent can be heavy. Tasha gets none of the benefits that some of her out-of-work friends are entitled to, although, thankfully, her local council provides free school meals to all children so that is one less thing to worry about.

The low point for Tasha was when she was receiving threatening calls and letters from her creditors at least once a day. As the main breadwinner and only reliable presence in her children's lives, she tried to hide her anxiety from everyone around her, directing it inwards, not knowing how or with whom to share her struggles. She acknowledges that this was a "dark time" and that she felt "very depressed, at times suicidal". Her nights were sleepless and her blood pressure soared. Scared to open letters, or the door for fear of who would be behind it, part of her knew that her debt collectors probably should not have been pursuing her in this way, but it was hard to know exactly what her rights were.

For Tasha, the greatest source of support – emotional, practical and, most importantly, financial – has been her parents. Although they have little money themselves, and no savings to draw on, they help out however they can. If the children needs shoes, clothes or a present for their birthday or Christmas, "nine times out of ten" Tasha turns to her parents. "We wouldn't have a Christmas if it wasn't for them."

But there is a downside to being financially reliant on loved ones. For a start, the psychological costs are substantial. And Tasha is acutely aware that her debt problems will be resolved when her parents die because she will inherit the bungalow in which they live and – thanks to its location – it is worth a considerable amount of money. But this fact causes her great pain: "When mum and dad go, I'll probably be comfortable then. But at what cost?"

What is more, it has always been Tasha's fervent hope that it would be *her* that provided for *them*, not the other way around. Having climbed the career ladder with such gusto, her cheeks redden (with shame? with anger?) at the thought of sliding back down again to such an extent that she has to turn to her elderly parents for help. But what else can she do?

There is hope in Tasha's story that she will pull through and emerge in the not-too-distant future from the financial turmoil that has defined her life for the last few years. In her eyes, the support that she has received from her parents has been fundamental, and she downplays her own resilience. But remarkable too is that, through her darkest times, she has managed to hang on to her job at the council and survive more than one round of redundancies. It begs the question of how a hard-working, aspirational single parent like her has been brought to the brink of a nervous breakdown by her children's participation in higher education. Extensive reforms to funding for universities – including the introduction of tuition fees and the replacement of maintenance grants with loans – has led to students from low-income families graduating with the highest debt levels, in excess of £57,000 (Belfield et al, 2017). In many ways, Tasha's children are precisely those who the expansion of university education is meant to benefit. Yet in her case, this has come at a significant personal and psychological cost.

FOURTEEN

The debt premium

Larissa Pople

Life is more expensive if you are living in poverty. The 'poverty premium' can take many guises. Fuel costs are higher for households that are not accessing the most economical tariff or cheapest billing method, and for those with pre-payment meters (Davies et al, 2016). Travel can cost more for those who cannot afford to run a car (Titheridge et al, 2014), and that is just considering the financial costs, never mind the time spent waiting at bus stops. Relatedly, food and shopping costs may be higher if you live in an area that does not have low-cost options, and cannot drive to somewhere that does (Davies et al, 2016). The list goes on. But many of the families we spoke to in our research were contending with the 'double whammy' of a 'debt premium' in addition to a poverty premium. Single mother Polly, and her two children – 13-year-old Ruby and 22-year-old Faith – were one such family.

Polly is well accustomed to managing the fragile balance between the amount of money going into her bank account and the amount going out. As a child, she grew up in a proud, "working-class poor" family, and as an adult, working part time as a healthcare assistant, she has never known anything other than being on a low income. So when, three years before our interview, she and Ruby moved into a council owned, two-bedroomed, Victorian conversion flat, Polly knew straight away that she needed to sort out some kind of payment plan for the fuel bills. Bitter experience had told her that, when you are close to the breadline, the smallest margin of error between expected and actual outgoings can be catastrophic. So she called up the energy provider and agreed an amount to pay each month. With the benefit of hindsight, she realises that the amount they suggested was far too low. "I was in cloud cuckoo land ... who in their right mind thinks that gas and electric costs £30 odd a month for God's sake?"

When the bill based on actual consumption came in three months later, she found that she owed £800, the equivalent of a whole month's salary. Part of the problem was that in comparison to her previous flat, which was purpose built and modern, it was nigh-on impossible to keep her new home warm. The high ceilings, expansive rooms and ill-fitting sash windows – all of the charming features of period properties that estate agents use to command high rents – meant that in the winter months, an icy draught would find its way in through the gaps and cracks, and whip through the house. Exposed floorboards and curtain-less windows only intensified the chill. By the time Polly realised how fast the gas meter was whirring to heat up the poorly insulated cavity that was her new home, the damage had been done. She found herself owing an "enormous sum of money" that she could not hope to pay off, and in arrears for the first time in her life.

Talking to the energy company about her options, she discovered that they were limited to three: pay the bill, be disconnected or have a pre-payment meter put in that would automatically take off a portion of the debt owing every time it is topped up. Choice was an illusion. The meter was put in and Polly had her first taste of the debt premium.

The premium associated with the pre-payment meter was substantial – an additional monthly cost for the dubious privilege of having the meter, higher rates of fuel because she was not paying by direct debit, and an inability to switch to a cheaper energy provider until she had cleared her debts.

'So you're the poorest in society. And you're paying more for your gas and electric. Because you had audacity to get into debt and you dared to owe them money, so it's like I've been fined, if you like, for being like that. So, you know, I've only got these meters in because I'm struggling. And as a result they've made me pay more.'

The fact that Polly's arrears related to her utilities has made them much harder to put out of her mind. Before the pre-payment meter was put in, and she was receiving bills threatening disconnection every other day, she would lie awake at night worrying that she would get up in the morning to find that they had been cut off. Now that she has the meter, she worries continuously that she has forgotten to top up the card, and that she will hear a 'beep beep beep' followed by the lights going off.

'It's sad really. Ruby will say: "Oh what's for dinner?" I say: "Oh just let me go and get my gas/electric first." I shouldn't be thinking of that first, I should be thinking of: "Oh let me go and get my shopping and get Ruby a couple of treats from Tesco's."'

At the risk of stating the obvious, families living in poverty are much more likely to be struggling with their utility bills than wealthier families: the rate of arrears on utilities is five times higher in households in poverty than it is in households that are not in poverty (JRF, 2015). What is more, if you are in a low-income household, you are more likely to be behind on your household bills than on consumer credit because many, like Polly, do not use consumer credit. Yet, although water cannot be cut off, and while it is unusual for gas and electricity to be disconnected, it is common for families facing difficulties to be switched to pre-payment meters, with the result that if you cannot afford to pay upfront, the supply is cut off.

Polly's two children have responded to the situation in their own ways. As in other families we have interviewed, debt affects siblings differently, a function of age, relationships, personality and other individual differences. Faith, always the problem solver, contributes to the household income whenever she can, and is able to do so as she has a full-time job. On a few occasions, when the amount that Polly can afford to put on the meter has not lasted the week, she has had to beg or borrow from friends and family, including from Faith, the particular premium associated with this debt being one of deep embarrassment:

> 'It's so embarrassing, you know, she's my daughter, you know what I mean? "Faith, have you got £10? My electric's going to go." "Oh right, I'll transfer it to your bank." You know. It's embarrassing. But I've had to do it, because, you know, me and Ruby have got to sit here in the pitch black otherwise.'

The impact on Ruby has been different. As Polly is taken up with the stress and logistics of ensuring that the electricity and gas do not turn off halfway through the week, she spends less time "just chatting" with her daughter like they used to, and Ruby spends more time in her bedroom. Recently, Ruby has been experiencing 'social anxiety' and has had several panic attacks, including on the bus into town with a friend one weekend, and during an exam at school. A bright and hard-working student, Ruby always used to skip off to school, but now she finds that on some days – she never knows when – the panic rises up within her and she is paralysed by a sense of all-encompassing anxiety.

It is clear that, in addition to the financial and psychological premiums associated with debt, Polly faces another premium that is under-recognised, yet equally important: time. Coping with problem debts is costly not just in monetary terms, but also in the number of hours spent worrying about and dealing with the situation.

When Polly and Ruby talk about the impact that the debt has had on relationships within the family, their words convey a deep-seated closeness between mother and daughter, but the debilitating stress caused by the ongoing struggle to keep the family finances afloat is also palpable. Increasingly, time is spent in different rooms: Ruby hidden away in her bedroom, and Polly bent over her laptop at the kitchen table, tapping furiously on the keyboard trying to eke out a few extra pounds here and there. When debt was not a problem, Polly would often spend time in the kitchen with Ruby sat next to her in quiet companionship reading a book or doing her homework. A cup of tea was shared, and morsels of conversation were exchanged. Now this tranquil slice of family life has been exchanged for something less serene.

FIFTEEN

Dreams

Sorcha Mahony

But I, being poor, have only my dreams;
I have spread my dreams under your feet;
Tread softly because you tread on my dreams.
(W.B. Yeats, 1899, Cloths of heaven, in *The wind
among the reeds*)

Amara Elwood has a dream. She is 14 years old and lives with her
mother, her occasional father, her three siblings and one of their
on-again-off-again boyfriends, in a three-bedroomed terraced house
on a large estate in the north of England. There is little furniture in
their home: no table in the dining room, just a two-seater sofa whose
corduroy cover is ripped and stained; no stand for the hand-me-down
television in the living room, just a collection of rag-tag cushions and
old blankets on the floor in front of it that double as a bed for Amara's
oldest sister and her sometimes-partner; and no bed in one of the
rooms upstairs, just a thin foam mattress on the laminate floor, which
has bubbled up around the leaky radiator pipes. There are no doors
or tyres on the car that lies rusting in the back yard, home to a rescue
puppy who is not yet house-trained and is banned from being indoors.

Sitting on a chrome and PVC chair in the middle of the kitchen, Amara thinks of her dream and smiles. She stops picking at the foam coming out of the chair seat, puts her hands under her thighs as if to contain them and looks me directly in the eye for the first time. The sparkle in hers seems to speak of a vision that is so much bigger than career aspiration or chosen vocational path; of a whole life imagined, conjured up out of the broken paving slabs and emptiness that characterise her neighbourhood and the material scarcity that marks her home. A future as somebody who matters.

Ever since she can remember, Amara has wanted to be a nurse. She says that she does not know where she got the idea from – it could have been from school, it could have been from the television, it could have been from the time she visited her nan in hospital after her kidney operation – she just knows that when she was little, at every opportunity she had to wear fancy dress, she would put on her little nurse's outfit and will the day when it would no longer be make-believe. She says that she would love to wear those smart blue scrubs and one of those little pocket watches for real, take people's temperatures, do their injections and help them get better. She's so proud of not being squeamish, that she did not flinch at the blood that came from her knee when she fell on some broken glass at the local recreation ground a few months previously.

But then she says: "That's not what I *will* be, it's just what I *want* to be." And as quick as it came, the glint in her eye – her dream – vanishes, replaced by the vacant stare from earlier, a shrug of the shoulders, a sigh that is barely audible. It is an *if I was somebody else* kind of dream; a dream of having a dream; a vision once-removed. She explains that her mother wanted to work in a dentist's once and that had come to nothing, so her notion of being a nurse will be similarly fated "I don't know, it just won't happen, anyway we probably won't have the money."

Amara knows that household finances are tight, and prohibitively so; that they currently live on benefits that do not cover the cost of the things they need; that one of her teachers bought her school uniform because her mother could not afford it; that her mother owes money to many people; and that they do not have enough money to go on holiday but instead spend the interminable weeks of summer at home – hungry, bored and getting on each other's nerves. She knows that her mother has credit cards and that she does not think that she will ever be able to pay back the debt on them. She was at home when the bailiffs came and her mother had happily let them in so they could see for themselves that there was nothing of value to take.

When she was younger, Amara's mother trained in food preparation and started out as a chef's assistant, working her way up the ranks towards the middle management of a catering company, although even then she relied on credit cards to cover the cost of things that her low wages did not. But her finances deteriorated quickly after she had three debilitating pregnancies, an abusive relationship with a man whose presence affected her benefit entitlements but whose main contribution was a wild and destructive temper, and went on to develop a host of mental health problems that left her scared to venture out of the house on her own for weeks on end, and unable to work. For the past few years she has bumped along that questionable line that separates the Have-Littles from the Have-Nots, with credit card debt a persistent feature on her financial landscape, stubborn in its refusal to rescind. A year before the interview, things became really difficult after she had an operation and ended up with an infection that left her hospitalised and distracted from her financial commitments. She relied on the credit cards to help with the cost of living – shoes for the children, credit for the mobile, petrol for the car before it broke down – and to try to make Christmases and birthdays ones for the children to remember. Her current financial situation seems complex, and I struggle to keep up as she talks through what she is entitled to in benefits (£204 a week in tax credits, £37 a week in Child Benefit, £64 a week in Employment and Support Allowance), what she pays out each week (£30 for electricity, £30 for gas, £50 for water, £30 towards rent and rent arrears, £10 for her phone, £45 for Amara and her older brother's and sister's "weekly money", £28 in Council Tax debt and about £120 for food) but then goes on to explain that her Tax Credits have been stopped since one of her sons stopped attending school, and her Housing Benefit is on hold pending an investigation into the status of her ex-partner within the house. She is hoping to get her benefits reinstated soon, with back-payments, as she is now in arrears with her rent (£320), Council Tax (£820) and television licence (£126), and has been to court for these and incurred even more costs in the process. She tries not to use her credit cards – the debt on them currently stands at around £12,000 – but sometimes, when the food parcels and handouts for gas and electricity are not forthcoming from the tenants' association or from the staff at Amara's school, she has no option. They are double-edged swords, allowing her to get by while other income sources are unavailable, but tethering her to a future of repayments.

For Amara's mother, who faces credit card debts that she believes will stretch well into the sixth decade of her life, the idea of seeing her daughter through nursing college is a remote and frankly unappealing prospect. Of course, she would love to see Amara happy and settled in a successful career as she moves into adulthood – what parent does not want this for their children – but she cannot be the one to provide the financial support for that endeavour. She is no stranger herself to curbing ambition, having been repeatedly priced out of her own dreams – first of training as a dental hygienist, then of setting up her own business and most recently of becoming an event planner – and she thinks that Amara will have to learn the hard way that the real limit to aspiration is money, not the sky.

For Amara, aware of her mother's thwarted ambitions, mindful of the cost of studying and wary of accruing debt, the prospect of becoming a nurse has ebbed and flowed with the tide of her mother's financial fortunes, but seems now perhaps more a fantasy than a dream; a place in her imagination she visits every now and then, or a convenient response when people ask her – as they always do – what she wants to do when she is older.

In the throes of poverty and debt, Amara and her mother have adjusted their dreams downwards, concerned mainly with the here and now of scraping by, and on the face of it this seems like a sensible response to the financial predicament they are in. It is just that they have done so to such a degree that they have all but abandoned the very things that once gave them hope and kept them going.

But we would be wrong to imagine that Amara and her mother are passive in the face of their curbed ambitions. To the contrary, they draw on a convincing narrative that allows them to cope with the reality of not only living, but dreaming, within their means. When I remark to Amara that it seems a shame to give up on her nursing idea, that she seemed so happy thinking about it earlier, she replies: "Well at least I'm not in jail." And she talks about a boy from the neighbourhood who is currently serving a six-year prison sentence and will not be out until Amara turns 17.

When I ask her mother how she copes with the strains of poverty and debt, and with the depression that medication never quite shifts, the anxiety that keeps her awake at night and the agoraphobia that prevents her from attending counselling sessions at the local community centre, she says that some people have it much worse, and when she thinks of that, it is easier to cope. It does not make the debts or poverty or other hardships go away, but it helps to know that things are not a whole lot tougher. And she talks about her best friend whose daughter died 18 months previously, her life now a memory, marked at home by an untouched bedroom and at the graveside by fresh flowers once a month and one of those helium balloons on her would-be birthday. Amara's mother says that even though things are hard, what with having no money and a stack of debts, at least her children are alive and she thanks her lucky stars for this.

"At least my children are alive." "At least I'm not in jail." Amara and her mother, along with some of our other participants, point readily to the extremes of human suffering in those around them – the bereavement, the suicide, the mental health problems, the childhood cancer, the bullying, the imprisonment – and tell themselves that things are not so bad in their own lives after all. And this may function as an effective psychological coping tactic, up to a point. But when that narrative is repeated often enough, when it is used time and again to paper over the cracks of a broken vision, it can come to eclipse that vision altogether until, again, people lose sight of the dreams they once held dear.

Hopes, visions, aspirations, dreams ... whatever we call them, they sit at the heart of the credit card industry, exploited in marketing and advertising campaigns for the hold they have over people's decisions and related financial behaviours. Without them, lenders would have little sway over their customers. Sometimes the dreams are modest and speak of the normalisation of poverty: a desire to make it through to payday, to pay off outstanding household bills, to replace a broken washing machine or to fix a burst water pipe. At other times they are made of bigger stuff: taking the trip of a lifetime, studying for higher education, financing a wedding or renovating a home. Big or small, credit card providers rely on people's dreams to encourage borrowing, tapping into the universal search for a better life to persuade would-be customers to engage with their products. And yet for some it is through this very borrowing that dreams can fall by the wayside, as poverty lingers, income shocks occur, debts become entrenched and the curbing of ambition passes down through the generations.

In July 2016, the Financial Conduct Authority (FCA) – the regulator for financial service firms and financial markets in the UK – reported on the findings of its Credit Card Market Study, a five-year study of over 34 million consumers (FCA, 2016). It showed, among other things, that there were around 30 million credit card holders in the UK at the time, and that 'around 3.3 million people are in persistent debt, with over half (1.8 million) for two consecutive periods of eighteen months' (FCA, 2017). It acknowledged that 'customers in persistent debt are profitable for credit card firms, who do not routinely intervene to help them' and that 'firms have few incentives' to help customers who are struggling financially (FCA, 2017).

In the spring of 2017, in recognition that a market-based solution to the problem of persistent credit card debt was unlikely, the FCA published a consultation paper proposing new measures designed to protect customers. The proposed rules would require credit card firms to take proactive steps in supporting customers to avoid persistent debt in the first place, to do more to prompt people to repay within a reasonable amount of time, to propose affordable repayment plans, and under certain circumstances to go further 'by reducing, waiving or cancelling any interest or charges' (FCA, 2017) and doing more to identify customers who are financially vulnerable. At the time of writing, the FCA was in the process of drawing up a policy statement in light of the feedback from its consultation, and updating its handbook of rules and guidance for the financial sector. For people like Amara's mother, who has all but abandoned the dream of living debt free, this could make a very real difference.

It is time to leave Amara's house – so that she and her mother can clean up after the puppy, which somehow found its way inside and managed to defecate on the floor, along the skirting and up one of the walls in the living room while we were talking. On the way out I see a clipping from a local newspaper lying on the kitchen counter, with a photograph of Amara under the headline 'Star Pupil Banks Brownie Points' – maybe this will provide an opportunity to end on a positive note? There has been little else in my visit to facilitate this. But when I ask about the article, Amara shrugs, although her mother beams and explains how Amara did so well on her work experience at the nearby branch of an international bank that the bank contacted the school and commended her hard work to the headteacher, who in turn phoned the local press and presented Amara with an achievement certificate and 50 house points. Amara's mother looks to her daughter as she ventures that working in a bank would make a good career as she would not have to pay to study first; she could just start earning as soon as she left school. But Amara snatches the clipping and says: "I hated it, it was the most boring week of my life." I leave the two of them arguing over what the future might hold, hoping that if I ever return there might be a set of blue scrubs with one of those little pocket watches hanging on the back of the kitchen door where Amara's school uniform is now. The cloths of her dream.

SIXTEEN

The gift[5]

Sorcha Mahony

The front door opens and a little pair of bright green feet appear at the threshold. The toes wiggle up and down before their owner Bobby jumps out, shouting "BOO" at the top of his voice. His mother Debbie laughs, explaining "oh he's been busy painting today" as she opens the door and leads the way to the lounge, pointing out the paint streaks on the wall as we go.

I give Debbie the packet of Hobnobs biscuits that I have brought and she asks one of her daughters to make tea, sending the other one off to the shop to top up the electricity meter. Participants often insist on making us tea when we arrive, the cultural ritual imbued with added layers of meaning in the context of material scarcity. So while 12-year-old Sian pops to the corner shop and nine-year-old Ella sorts the drinks out, Debbie and I settle down on the sofa, little Bobby raiding his toy box as she talks through who lives in the house and what they do.

They are a family of five. Debbie works as an adviser for a drugs rehabilitation charity and her husband Rich works as a night-time delivery driver for a fast-food chain. They have three children: Sian who is in Year 7 at school, Ella who is in Year 5 and two-year-old

Bobby, "our happy little accident". Hearing his name, Bobby toddles over with his pull-along plastic telephone, picks up my tea and polishes off the entire cup before climbing onto my knee and settling down in my lap, where he remains, dozing, for the duration of the interview.

Debbie and Rich always had stable salaries, except during a brief period of unemployment when the delivery company Rich worked for went into administration and it took him a few weeks to find another job. While not particularly high earners, they felt financially secure, and for a long time did not experience or think of their debts as problematic: they were a two-salary household with a joint income of around £2,700 a month so although they relied on overdrafts, loans, store cards and a hire-purchase scheme for their car, they knew there was money coming in to make the repayments on their debts in addition to covering the household bills. In Debbie's mind they were a fully working household, and if their combined salaries did not cover the cost of the things they felt this entitled them to, then they would just have to borrow money to make up the difference. Debbie and Rich were determined to give their children the things they felt they deserved – annual visits to family abroad, outings at the weekend, a computer, a few nice clothes – and to make their home comfortable, warm and welcoming.

This approach worked for years. "And then my son arrived and I went onto maternity leave and statutory maternity pay, and I realised that we couldn't afford to pay everything." In the haze of nappies and sleepless nights, Debbie's grip on the household finances loosened. Her income was down by £800 a month and they had no savings. Things were tight for a while. They shopped stringently and stopped all non-essential expenditure. They began to use credit cards for everyday living. They juggled which debt they prioritised each month, rotating payments for the car, the loan for the dining room furniture and the store card accounts. Rich and Debbie withdrew from each other. Debbie went back to work – earlier than she had planned to – and put Bobby into nursery full time. But while the household income returned to its previous level, they now had almost £1,000 a month in nursery fees to pay and debts that were starting to feel too big. Aspects of everyday life began to take on new meanings: instead of seeing the dining room furniture and remembering the family gatherings they had hosted around it, Debbie saw the burden of the debt it contained; and self-doubt crept in when she thought back to some of the family trips they had taken, casting a shadow over the fond memories she once enjoyed. Christmas was a few months away and Debbie and Rich agreed to get through it and then seek advice in the new year on how to get back on track. She would look into getting childcare vouchers for Bobby's nursery fees, see if they were eligible for more in tax credits, maybe go to counselling with Rich to try to work things out. She was prepared to do whatever it took – get rid of the car, stop the holidays, possibly even move somewhere cheaper. They would just give the children one last Christmas before the purse strings would really tighten.

In October, Debbie received a letter from the local authority. It said that she had missed a Council Tax payment for £90 and that she now owed the full amount for the remainder of the financial year in one lump sum – around £700. She called the council, apologised for the error, explained that she had a lot on and asked to pay in instalments, as she had always done. She was told that she would have to pay in full as she had not responded to the reminder notice and had thereby forfeited the option to pay in instalments. No exceptions. Debbie did not dispute that she owed the money, but explained that she had not seen a reminder notice and that she needed to spread the cost of the bill:

'I rang up and said: "Look I'm really struggling at the moment, this is me trying to be open, transparent about it all." But it was like … nope … I don't know, say you've got a debt with Provident or whatever, they're very much send you letters, send you letters, send you letters, phone you up, sort it out, but with Council Tax it's like one letter came and within weeks it went to the bailiffs.'

One evening, a few weeks after receiving the letter, Debbie and the girls were watching television when the doorbell rang. Two bailiffs stood on the front path "obnoxious, nasty men, tried to do the scare tactics", cameras attached to the breast pockets of their jackets, filming everything. They explained that they had come to collect the money owed for the Council Tax and that Debbie had to let them in.

'I said: "You are not coming in." "Oh we have to", he said. So I said: "No you don't, you need to go and get the police if you want forced entry." The way they went about it all is absolutely disgusting. There are some very, very vulnerable people out there and have got bailiffs knocking on the door within weeks of getting the first letter.'

Debbie shook for hours afterwards and told her daughters that from now on they were never, ever to open the front door to anyone.

November came and Debbie was due to get paid at the end of the month. They desperately needed the money to top up the gas and electricity meters as the weather had turned cold and Rich's wages had gone straight towards the rent and nursery fees. It felt like a long couple of weeks before payday, but then when it came, instead of the expected £1,400, Debbie received just under £300. She called her employer to find out what was going on and they told her they had received an Attachment of Earnings Order – an instruction from the local authority to pay the outstanding balance on Debbie's Council Tax bill, in full, direct from her wages. She phoned the council, asked to be repaid in full and to spread the cost so that she would not be left without money in the run-up to Christmas, and asked why the money taken exceeded what she owed in Council Tax. The Council Tax adviser said that the decision was irreversible and that the amount taken from her wages (£1,100) was higher than the Council Tax bill because it included the cost of the bailiffs and court proceedings.

'They literally didn't give, excuse me I am going to swear now, they didn't give an absolute shit at all that I had children. I told them: "I have children.". I told them I was prepared to go forward with a debt management plan, but the way they worded it was "you've done this yourself, you've got yourself into this, you get yourself out". Apparently they sent me a letter to try and get an overview of my earnings, but I didn't see any letter, then they automatically assumed, they assumed I earned a top-whack wage or something and they went and got an order and they just took the money out of my wage. It is like a wages order, where they just go into your wages and take it. They went straight to the wages department and took it.'

Debbie says that the council may well have sent a reminder notice and a letter asking for a summary of her earnings, but she had so much going on that it could have slipped under her radar as she and Rich juggled full-time work, the children, their relationship and sorting out their other debts. She was prepared to accept full responsibility for her mistake, and apologised for it, but was still not allowed to spread the cost of the Council Tax bill. With the benefit of hindsight, she sees that they had been living beyond their means for years, but she had resolved to address their debts in the new year, and believes that the way the Council Tax debt was dealt with was unnecessarily punitive and achieved nothing.

In 2014, the year Debbie and Rich fell foul of the local authority's tax collection system, there were an estimated 920,000 families in England with arrears on their Council Tax bills, with 1.6 million children living in these households (The Children's Society, 2015b). Up until April 2013, households with low incomes that struggled to pay bills received Council Tax Benefit – a national scheme designed to provide support for the most financially vulnerable among us. But in April 2013, the government replaced Council Tax Benefit with new, localised schemes for providing Council Tax support, and for many families this meant a reduction in the amount of financial assistance they received for making their Council Tax payments. As The Children's Society reported in its publication *Wolf at the door*, research by the Local Government Association 'found that only 45 out of 326 councils continue to provide the same level of discount that was available under the old scheme' (The Children's Society, 2015b, p 12).

In 2014, there were also no special considerations for families with children who fell into arrears, and no statutory guidance governing how local authorities should collect Council Tax debts, and this is still the case at the time of writing. While the FCA regulates the debt recovery practices of consumer lenders, no such regulatory framework exists for government lenders, and councils are within their rights to demand an entire year's tax from people who miss a monthly instalment, while the courts can send bailiffs to their homes and take money direct from their bank accounts, wage packets or benefits, within weeks of a missed payment, regardless of whether there are children living in the house and irrespective of the potential effects on them. Councils have a duty of care for the wellbeing of their residents, but it seems that this is easily forgotten in the context of debts owed: falling into problem debt to a local authority appears to eclipse people's status as citizens, who have a right to support in times of need. It is not yet clear whether the Breathing Space scheme announced by the government in October 2017 will apply to Council Tax debt.

In 2014, Debbie and Rich cancelled Christmas: they did not give presents and they ate a normal dinner. They told extended family that they had come down with a bug and for the first time in years their house was quiet on Christmas Day. They told the girls that Christmas was postponed as they were not feeling well and that they would hopefully have a belated celebration in the new year. Somehow, pretending that it was not happening seemed easier than trying to celebrate without the means to really do so. On the advice of a friend in whom Debbie had confided, they contacted Citizens Advice, which signposted them to StepChange Debt Charity, with whom they are now working through their options, and they are considering filing for bankruptcy. It is hard for them to see how else they will get on top of the £26,000 that they owe.

I ask Debbie about the effects of the debts and from her response it seems that they have been many and far-reaching, touching on a fundamental sense of personal and parental competence, self-worth and dignity. And one of the hardest ways this manifests is through the family's ability to give – to themselves and to each other but especially to extended family and friends. "I've deprived myself," Debbie says.

'In not eating … it's like cereal rather than a meal and stuff like that. I'm aware that it's horrible, but that's had to happen … I don't know if it's our Italian background or something, but we like our food and dinner was a big thing. And we used to always have a lot of the family round but we can't do that anymore. Cousins used to come round and share Sunday dinner with us and we can't, you know I dread it when they come because I've got nothing to give them. And that I find awful. So, in a way I avoid, I try not to have them around, which is dreadful, because then I'm breaking up the family.'

In their daughter Sian's interview later – also conducted on the sofa while Bobby continues to doze in my lap and Debbie gets dinner ready in the kitchen – it is clear that she is aware of the Council Tax debt, if not the full picture of indebtedness and financial insecurity:

'I know we get short of money because of Council Tax.… Usually I hear my mum and dad talking about it, about not having enough money to feed us and everything because like the food is harder to put all around on the table so we're not getting that much anymore as we used to. Mainly I usually eat at school but I don't eat that much at school because there's a massive line, like about a hundred people in the line, two hundred people, and I'm usually at the very back so there's nothing left.… And there weren't presents last year because we had to pay the Council Tax a lot more.'

And it is clear too that Sian feels the inability to give as keenly as her mother. She talks about a friend's birthday party and how she did not go because she had nothing to give to her friend: "Mum said to go anyway and just tell her I forgot the present and I'll bring it to school next week and that. But I didn't want to do that so I just didn't go."

The constraints on giving manifest in different ways for different participants. For some young people it is about knowing that you could not pay your friends back if they offer to buy your cinema ticket, so not going to the movies, or about not being able to take your turn buying hot chocolate at McDonald's, so making excuses when your friends invite you to go with them. For some parents it is about not being able to buy a round of drinks at the pub or give presents for birthdays or Christmas, or about not allowing the children to have friends over because every single penny is allocated to repaying debts. And alongside the effects this can have on social relationships – resulting in the unwitting transgression of the deep-seated cultural norm of reciprocity, or in social withdrawal – it can eat away at the very essence of a person, at their self-esteem, their sense of competence and their feelings of entitlement to live with dignity and respect. Not giving might be a coping tactic, and one of the few ways open to those in problem debt to exercise some agency in their situation, but it is one that carries in its wake a host of negative outcomes – social and psychological – and they cut deep and last long.

Sian's interview finishes and Debbie calls out that tea is ready. Sian goes to the kitchen and comes back with two plates of food – one for me and one for her. Given what they have both just said about not having the money to feed themselves properly let alone host others, this is uncomfortable. Should I accept the food knowing there is already not enough to go around and knowing more specifically that Debbie will not eat dinner tonight, or decline and risk offending them, risk withholding a potential opportunity for them to restore a feeling of capability and sense of self? I take the food – a burger with no bun and three slices of tomato – and Debbie prizes Bobby out of my lap. He whinges and whimpers and once he is gone it transpires that the warm patch on my lap has not come from his body heat after all, but is Bobby's own special little present to me – my cup of tea, drunk by him and redelivered onto my trousers. His parting gift to take its place alongside the other unexpected offerings from participants in these interviews – the impromptu dinners, a plastic picture frame, a wooden spice rack, a drawing of SpongeBob SquarePants. All of them, expressions of generosity but also of the importance of giving to others in fully realising ourselves.

SEVENTEEN

Our participants

Sorcha Mahony

In the stories for this book, our focus has been on the difficulties that our research participants have experienced in light of problem debt and poverty, and for most (adults), these issues did indeed seem to loom large in everyday life. But there is so much more to their lives than the financial vulnerability we have focused on here, so much that they contribute to the world around them – to their families, to their communities and to wider society. In fact, a key refrain to emerge from our debt research is the need people feel to be respected, to be seen not in terms of their financial circumstances alone and the deficit that defines these but in terms of the whole of themselves, and especially their achievements – their qualifications, their jobs, their voluntary work, their hobbies and interests, and their aspirations for the future. In an effort to respect this need, here we briefly recount some of the achievements, accolades and contributions that abound in our participants' collective profile. We ask ourselves what we saw beyond debt and financial hardship when we visited our participants, when we dipped into their lives for the briefest of moments.

We saw people with GCSEs, O Levels, A Levels, Bachelors degrees (for example in housing law and education management), Masters degrees (including in business administration) and, in one case, a PhD.

We saw health workers, local government employees, administrators in the private, charitable and public sectors, office managers, childminders, lecturers, army officers, yoga instructors, housing support workers, taxi drivers, tilers, engineers, bank clerks, drug and alcohol support workers, waitresses, full-time carers, party entertainers, sales assistants, chefs, security guards, teachers, facilities managers, customer services operatives, factory workers, forklift truck drivers, bar attendants, student counsellors, school nurses, outreach dementia workers, cleaners, kitchen porters, oncology nurses, builders, clinical research nurses, learning support assistants, outboard motor technicians, social workers, naval officers, internet retailers, minibus drivers, hod carriers, secretaries, business development managers, entrepreneurs in the renewable energy industry, delivery drivers, garden centre assistants, meals-on-wheels coordinators, volunteer coordinators and healthcare assistants. And we saw people who volunteer as community activists, church wardens, family support workers and school governors.

We saw young people with passion and talent for physical education, creative writing, technology, maths, religious studies, art, photography, music, fashion and design, cricket, boxing, football, rugby, film noir, trampolining, snooker and collecting vintage zoo brochures.

And we saw aspiring college and university students, future lawyers, psychologists, nurses, dancers, plumbers, IT managers, nursery school teachers, veterinary assistants, beauty therapists, artists, journalists and authors.

Most of all we saw children, young people and parents doing the best they can in challenging circumstances, living each day for nothing more than to enjoy the same kinds of lives as those they see around them. And at times we saw the remarkable tenacity of hope, of optimism and positivity, and a belief in the idea that one day things will get easier. In the words of one of our young participants:

'A day without a smile is like snow without water.'

Concluding reflections

Sorcha Mahony

Research reflections

Throughout this book, our brief methodological reflections were intended to be peripheral to the substantive stories – passing nods to some of the details involved in undertaking social research that are less well documented in methodology textbooks, and which can take novice researchers by surprise and keep more experienced ones on their toes. Nonetheless, we believe it is worth recapping on these and drawing out the overall methodological lessons we have been reminded of during our debt research, as they may be useful for readers embarking on similar studies.

The first of these lessons concerns the relationship of the researcher to those whose lives and experiences she intends to investigate. As noted in 'The journey' (Chapter One), there is a view that those studying the social world should not intervene in that world, but should keep a distance so as to ensure a measure of 'objectivity'. While the idea of researchers becoming deeply involved in the setting of their research has long been at the heart of ethnography, much social research outside of the ethnographic tradition still tries to adhere to the principles of distance and 'objectivity'.

In this book, we have taken a different viewpoint. On ethical and epistemological grounds, we believe that it is when we relate closely to participants, transgressing the boundaries of much received wisdom around non-intervention in the field, that we can be of most use – to participants themselves, but also to the quality of the data we collect and thereby to the field of knowledge we are trying to contribute to. Did Larissa intervene when she ran to the shops after Ruth's interview and bought dinner for the family? Yes. Do we intervene and thereby influence things when we turn up offering biscuits and give high-street shopping vouchers when interviews have finished? Yes. Are we already influencing things at recruitment stage by explaining to potential participants that we work for a charity that exists to understand and support vulnerable young people and their families, in part through using our research data in our lobbying work? Again, yes. Did I influence things when, as recounted in 'Dreams' (Chapter Fifteen), I inadvertently stirred up an argument between Amara and her mother as I left? Definitely. Did I influence things when I struggled to end Tom's interview on a positive note, in 'The tyranny of the small things' (Chapter Eleven)? Yes, and he spent the next couple of minutes trying to reassure *me* that he and his family would be okay. Do these interventions invalidate our data somehow? No, they make them the products of human interactions, which in themselves can reveal further insights: Tom's ability to see a silver lining, the poverty-related tensions between Amara and her mother as well as the love, Ruth's relief at being able to feed her children and possibly at being understood. Would we influence things anyway, just differently, even if we did not make these kinds of interventions? Yes.

The fact is that we all influence things in some way, however minimally, when we are present in a situation, whether as researchers, family members, colleagues, friends or even strangers. And given this, we believe that a good approach to take in a research context is to acknowledge our presence and point, where relevant, to the ways in which this might affect the data we have collected. It is possible that in response to our interventions, participants may feel more obliged to tell us things they think we want to hear ('researcher bias'). But we heard such a range of views and experiences during our fieldwork that it is hard to see how everyone's narratives could have been geared towards trying to please us in some way. Some of the things our participants told us surprised us, as they contravened socially accepted norms (see, for example, 'The elephant in the room' [Chapter Six] and Kevin's plans to borrow yet more money despite the considerable debt he already owes) or revealed a level of destitution that many would opt to conceal – see, for example, Sian's narrative in 'The gift' (Chapter Sixteen). It is also possible that by intervening as we have done, as opposed to just observing, we entrench a power imbalance between researcher and participant, reinforcing a notion of participants as unable to fend for themselves. However, on the whole, people showed few signs of feeling unequal to us in any way (with the possible exception of some of our younger, shyer participants); rather, they received our offerings, sometimes expressed gratitude for the time we had taken to listen to their stories, offered us things in return, and in many cases spoke with pride about the ways they had succeeded in life despite the challenges they faced.

The second lesson we have been reminded of in our debt research concerns the importance of keeping an open mind, and of scrutinising the judgements we do – inevitably – make. There are two elements to this lesson. First, it entails keeping an open mind about the *ways* in which people tell their stories. For some, this might be over the telephone – see 'Who cares?' (Chapter Five) – while for others it might be in public rather than at 'home' – see 'Loss' (Chapter Three) and the meeting with Alex in a station café, which later transpired to be related to the fact that he and his son were living in a hostel. Some people tell their stories using few very words – see 'Isolation' (Chapter Two) and George's economical approach to speaking – while for others, a story might be told through their *absence* from the research sample – see 'Keeping up appearances' (Chapter Nine). The way people tell their stories can teach us a lot: about the people themselves, the situations they have found themselves in, and the ways they respond to those situations; and about our own assumptions regarding optimal data collection, and sometimes about the broader context in which people's narratives can be located.

The second element in this lesson concerns the importance of keeping an open mind about participants themselves, about their choices and related behaviours. With the concepts of poverty and debt so heavily infused with strong (and dichotomous) assumptions within public discourse – with those labelled 'poor' and 'indebted' often either vilified or pitied – it was sometimes difficult to know how to see and tell things without falling into the trap of what sociologist Lois Wacquant calls the 'eager embrace of the clichés of public debate' – *'sanitizing'*, *'dichotomizing'* or *'glamorizing'* people's behaviours and decisions (Wacquant, 2002, p 1469). Here we were reminded of the importance of including the issues that stood out for us, even if these were unpalatable or if they problematised the image of 'problem debt' or the 'deserving poor', but to locate these within their broader – psychological, discursive and structural – contexts. And so, for example, we *did* include stories where levels of debt were relatively small, although this situation may not resonate with dominant notions about the point at which debts become 'problematic' – see, for example, 'Who cares?' (Chapter Five). We *did* include reference to participants smoking and drinking, to the Sky packages they subscribe to, and to the continued consumerism despite lack of personal funds, although these potentially play right into the widespread, pejorative narratives of 'feckless scroungers' and the 'immorally indebted'. But we also pointed to the wider moralising discourses that condemn these behaviours, and to the broad structures that at the same time legitimise, or even require, them: consumerism, the advertising industry that supports it, and the credit industry that pushes people towards it. We *did* describe some of the less charitable opinions expressed by our participants – see in particular 'The Others' (Chapter Eight) – because we wanted to show that our participants are human like the rest of us, and again we pointed to the discursive and structural contexts that can facilitate these opinions. We *did* include our observations of some of the less pleasant aspects of everyday life we encountered – the urine-infused stairwells, the dog faeces, the bedraggled front gardens, the arguments and the allusions to violence – despite the potential pitfall of reinforcing an image of participants as culturally and morally 'corrupt'. But we did this in the context of pointing to the overwhelming pressures that leave no time or energy for humouring the expectations of polite society; and further, we have described participants who do not fit this mould, who inhabit other social and cultural worlds – see, for example, 'Isolation' (Chapter Two) and 'Juggling' (Chapter Twelve) – yet *still* find themselves living in the debt trap. In short, we have been reminded of the importance of trying to understand those aspects of the indebted life that seem to invite such quick and easy judgement from others, by facing them head on and locating them within the web of forces – social, psychological, moral and economic – that surround them.

There is a view (often implicit), perhaps especially strong within the charity sector, that the stories we tell about our research participants should be constructed such that they provide no additional fodder for the pernicious discourse of the 'undeserving poor'. This is understandable – there is already enough contempt out there for some of the people whose voices we try to project, so why add fuel to the fire? However, we believe that there is room for more nuanced understandings, and that by including accounts that reveal some of the complexities, contradictions and unwitting adherence to stereotypes, and by locating these observations and narratives within the contexts that give them meaning, we are better equipped to more fully understand the life of problem debt and how it might be addressed.

The third and final lesson we have been reminded of in undertaking this research is the importance of building a network of peers to whom we can turn when we face ethical dilemmas, when we struggle to make sense of the sometimes unwieldy data we collect, and when our encounters with participants leave us at a loss as to how our research might be of use. As noted in 'Loss' (Chapter Three), the social research profession currently has no formal structure that allows researchers to work through the emotional – and we might add ethical, analytical and process-oriented – struggles we encounter, and in the absence of such a formal structure we must invent our own. Such networks could also function as forums within which to admit when we are wrong so that we properly learn the lessons our participants teach us – see the ending of 'The Child' (Chapter Ten) – to acknowledge the times we neglect to ask pertinent questions, to discuss our own feelings of guilt in the context of our research encounters – see 'Guilt' (Chapter Seven) – to share some of the more bizarre elements of our experience (for example, being weed on during an interview and being spoken to in an imitation American accent) and to figure out what to do with all the things people tell us that are not so easily incorporated into our research reports – see 'Juggling' (Chapter Twelve) and the positive effect of problem debts on Maryam and Said's relationship with each other and with their children. Whatever the particular issues we might bring to it, having access to a network of supportive peers is invaluable in enabling reflective research practice, and through this, producing research outputs that do justice to the stories that people share with us and the contexts within which they have come to be told.

Theoretical reflections

It has not been our intention with this book to write a theoretical treatise. Rather, while making our theoretical underpinnings transparent so that readers know the conceptual framework that has influenced our interpretation of the data, we always intended these to take a back seat to the empirical stories themselves. Nonetheless, many of the stories in this book speak to the concepts of agency and structure – and to the theory of 'negative agency' – and so it is worth revisiting this discussion briefly here, for readers who are interested in the theoretical side of things.

Our basic theoretical position is that individuals – children, young people and adults, including those living in highly constrained circumstances – exercise agency; that is, they have the capacity to make choices and act in the world (although clearly, there are differences between individuals and groups in this regard). At the same time, the social world is made up of structures – the economic, social and cultural institutions, norms, values and traditions that are relatively slow-changing (such as the family, government, the media and the credit industry, to name a few). One of the key debates in the social sciences is over the primacy of agency or structures, that is, over whether structures dictate the social world and people's behaviours and choices in it, or whether individuals determine their own fates and shape structures. Several theories have been proposed that aim to avoid the essentialising and dichotomous tendencies within the 'agency versus structure' debate, taking account of the ways in which agency and structures are interlinked and mutually constitutive (Giddens' 1984 structuration theory and Bourdieu's 1996 theories of social and cultural (re)production can be understood as examples of this).

In the 1980s – at around the same time as these broad theoretical debates were being played out in the social sciences – a new sub-field of enquiry had begun to emerge, known as the 'new social studies of childhood'. Developed in light of a perception that social scientific enquiry paid insufficient attention to children and young people as agents (with the capacity to reflect on their own lives and be research participants themselves), the central concern of this body of knowledge became to document the ways in which children and young people exercise agency, using methods that sought to elicit testimony from the children and young people themselves. While the 'new social studies of childhood' succeeded in highlighting the fact that children and young people exercise agency, it also stopped short of exploring the ways in which that agency comes into contact with the structures that surround it.

In response to the perceived absence of critical engagement with children and young people's agency within the new social studies of childhood, certain scholars within anthropology and human geography (such as Jane Dyson and Craig Jeffrey) – especially those exploring the lives of young people living in the 'global south' – began to pay more attention to what Jeffrey (2011, p 245) has labelled 'negative agency': to the ways in which agency can have harmful and counterproductive effects when exercised from positions of structural marginalisation. For example, within my own research into the lives of young people living in slum communities in Bangkok, I found that although the people I studied exercised agency in numerous ways, their efforts in one realm of life would often undermine their endeavours and chances of success in other spheres, because they engaged with structures on such disadvantaged terms (Mahony, 2018).

In short, over the past few decades, within broad sociological debates and within the more focused fields of childhood and global youth studies, there has been increasing recognition of the complexities that exist at the interface of agency and structures, and specifically an impetus to seek out the ways in which agency might become 'negative' when exercised from positions of structural disadvantage.

In the context of this book, we have come to understand much of our data on problem debt through this theoretical lens of negative agency – as this applies to adults as well as young people. While this is more prominent in some stories, we found time and again that it was a useful tool in helping us to think through what might be going on in any given debt scenario, and that in some cases it provided a way of potentially linking together what appeared at first sight to be unrelated issues. In 'The journey' (Chapter One), we showed how Ruth exercised agency to ensure that her rent was paid so that she and her children had a roof over their heads, but how, given her low income, this meant (re)accruing other debts, which led to a feeling of long-term insecurity and a bad credit rating. In 'Isolation' (Chapter Two), we showed how Stella exercised agency in an attempt to repay her debts, but how, because she was "working, always working", her son George was left to his own devices and had found refuge in a virtual world, where he was increasingly exposed to online violence. In 'The Others' (Chapter Eight), we showed how Sally (and to a lesser extent her children) invoked the discourse of the 'immorally indebted' as a psychosocial survival tactic, but how – while she may have gained a felt moral advantage in the process – she also contributed to keeping the pernicious narrative alive, for others to use against her. In 'Keeping up appearances' (Chapter Nine), we demonstrated the lengths to which Sandra goes to hide her problem debts from everyone around her, but how this in turn means that she perpetuates an unsustainable spending pattern and lives with an unsustainable level of stress. In 'The tyranny of the small things' (Chapter Eleven), we highlighted the myriad little ways in which Tom restrains his consumption at home in an effort to free up household resources for repaying debts, but how these efforts result in a life half lived, which in turn contributes to him feeling like a failure in life. In 'The debt premium' (Chapter Fourteen), we saw how Polly borrowed money from family members – including her grown-up daughter – to repay debts, but how this led to deep feelings of shame in her. In 'Dreams' (Chapter Fifteen), we showed how Amara and her mother had put a hold on their ambitions in the face of poverty and debt, and made themselves feel a bit better by invoking the narrative that 'things could be worse', but how this functioned to eclipse the dreams that once gave them hope. And in 'The gift' (Chapter Sixteen), we saw how Debbie had restricted the household budget in order to repay debts such that the family could no longer afford to give to others, but how this led to a fracturing of the family and of a sense of self.

The examples are numerous, but what they demonstrate is the same: that exercising agency can only get you so far – and can have unintended, negative consequences – if you are positioned at the wrong end of the socioeconomic inequality spectrum. In 'Who cares?' (Chapter Five), Steven told us that "there's only so many times you can redo a budget if there's not enough money in it". We have found something similar in a theoretical sense: there are only so many ways you can exercise agency before it starts to turn back on itself and undermine its own efforts, if it is poorly positioned in relation to structural constraints, and especially if those structures are multiple.

Policy reflections and recommendations

So, given the severe structural obstacles that people face living with problem debt, and given that they are already exercising varying degrees of agency trying to escape its clutches, or trying to fulfil some other requirement of them (to be ideal consumers, to be credit-card holders, to be perfect parents, to be like their peers at school), what might be done to support them? Much of the discussion in this section was developed with the help of Sam Royston and is based on his book *Broken benefits: What's gone wrong with welfare reform* (Royston, 2017).

Poverty and welfare reform

As the stories in this book demonstrate, the underlying issue of low income drives many families' experiences of problem debt, in some cases making it harder to save for a sudden additional cost, in other cases meaning that families are unable to afford day-to-day essentials, resulting in them falling behind with utility bills or borrowing money to cover the cost of food or clothes. What these families need is a secure, stable and adequate income with which to raise their children.

However, in recent years, social security provision has been reduced considerably, and this is likely to continue. At the time of writing, around four million children live in poverty, and this is expected to reach five million by 2020 (Hood and Waters, 2017). Benefit freezes, reductions in disability support, reductions in in-work support, cuts to support for new parents – all of these measures function to diminish incomes, making it even harder for some families to avoid problem debt.

Benefit freezes

Since 2010, benefit entitlements have increased below the rate of inflation, or they have been frozen altogether. Child Benefit – which David Cameron called 'one of the most important benefits there is' – has been particularly hard hit by this below-inflationary uprating (Mason, 2015). As things stand, Child Benefit will have risen by just 2% over the course of the current decade – one 17th of the expected increase in prices (Royston, 2017, p 104). In 'Keeping up appearances' (Chapter Nine), we saw how Sandra struggled to manage the cost of living for her family, despite accessing the benefits they were entitled to. Similarly, in 'The tyranny of the small things' (Chapter Eleven), we learned how Tom, his siblings and their mother lived a life of frugality that seemed to belong to a different era, because the household income simply did not cover their outgoings and debt repayments. In 'Dreams' (Chapter Fifteen), we saw how the income in Amara's household did not stretch to cover the cost of living, and how her family relied on the generous but ad-hoc support of teachers at school and the local residents' association to pay for clothes, food and electricity. In each of these cases – and in others in this book – having a level of children's benefits that rose in line with the cost of living could really help.

Similarly, many families have been affected by rents rising faster than increases in support with housing costs. Until recently, the Local Housing Allowance (LHA) – which determines the amount of Housing Benefit that people renting in the private rental sector receive – was based on average rents and increased in line with rises in local rent levels. This ensured that as local rents rose, people could continue living in their own communities – and continue drawing support from the social networks they had built up around them, keep their children settled at local schools and, in many cases, continue in local jobs.

However, from 2013, the government made a number of changes to the way LHA is set. Instead of increasing LHA rates in line with local rents, it decided to limit increases in LHA rates in line with the Consumer Price Index (CPI) measure of inflation. This was followed by a decision to further restrict LHA rises to no more than 1% for two years (with exceptions for the fastest-rising rents through a Targeted Assistance Fund). As a result of this (and other changes), LHA rates no longer bear any relationship to typical local rents, meaning that for many families there is a substantial gap between their maximum Housing Benefit entitlement and their actual rent. The government's own evaluation of LHA reforms (DWP, 2014) found that, faced with the prospect of tenants experiencing these kinds of shortfalls, some landlords said that they were attempting to stop renting to Housing Benefit claimants. Nearly half of landlords renting to people receiving LHA said that they had seen an increase in rent arrears, and one in five said that they have taken action to evict tenants because of the impact of the LHA reforms.[6]

In 'Loss' (Chapter Three), we met Alex, who struggled with rent payments following the death of his son Max, his wife's subsequent departure and his own struggle with mental ill-health, all of which entailed a reduction in household income. In this story we saw Alex and his remaining son Joseph placed in a hostel, after being notified of an impending rent increase that Alex knew he could not afford, and after an aborted attempt at living with his mother in her overcrowded, one-bedroomed flat. For families who have experienced a reduction in income and rent increases (let alone the type of tragedy that befell Alex and Joseph), housing support that reflected the actual rents they are due to pay, could make a real difference to their capacity to keep a roof over their heads. It serves nobody's best interests for children and their parents to languish in temporary accommodation.

Reductions in disability benefits

As a number of stories in this book show, ill-health or disability can be a key driver of families falling into problem debt. This is evident in: 'Loss' (Chapter Three), wherein Alex was unable to work for a while after Max's death due to the mental health problems he experienced, and in 'The elephant in the room/consumerism' (Chapter Six), wherein Jill developed Type II diabetes and was forced to stop work. It can also be seen in 'Keeping up appearances' (Chapter Nine), wherein Sandra's husband had to give up work after he was diagnosed with a chronic heart condition and in 'Juggling' (Chapter Twelve), wherein Said developed multiple sclerosis, was eventually unable to work and had to make extensive modifications to the family home. We saw it too in 'Dreams' (Chapter Fifteen), wherein Amara's mother first had three debilitating pregnancies, then an operation that left her hospitalised, and subsequently developed a host of mental health problems that severely affected her ability to function in the outside world.

What families like these need is support to make up the shortfall between their reduced incomes due to the illnesses and disabilities they experience, and their continued financial commitments. However, recent policy changes present further challenges for them. For example, entitlements for many people claiming Employment and Support Allowance – the key benefit received by those unable to work as a result of ill-health – have been substantially reduced.

Similarly, for disabled people who are able to work (as Said from 'Juggling' in Chapter Twelve was in the early days of his multiple sclerosis), changes associated with the introduction of Universal Credit significantly reduce the amount of in-work support designed to help them with the additional costs they face working. In some cases, families with a disabled worker could lose over £50 a week as a result of these changes.

For families who experience chronic illness or disability, whether they continue to work or have to stop working altogether, having these reductions reversed could make the difference between problematic and manageable debt.

Reductions in in-work benefits

Low-income working families also often struggle to cover the cost of living even when there is no disability or illness in the household. Indeed, this is evident in most of the stories in this book. What low-income working families need is additional income that makes up the difference between what they earn and what they must pay out for the cost of living. However, recent changes have significantly reduced some forms of in-work support.

When Universal Credit was first developed, it was designed to provide support for people to move into work through the provision of 'work allowances' – amounts of earnings that working claimants could keep before additional earnings started to affect their benefit entitlement. In 2016, the government reduced the value of these work allowances. Before the changes, a single claimant receiving Universal Credit could earn £111 a month before additional earnings started to affect their Universal Credit entitlement. After the changes, they couldn't earn anything at all without it affecting their entitlements. This cut in work allowance reduces support for working single parents who own their own home by £212 a month (£2,544 per year). For people like Stella from 'Isolation' (Chapter Two) – a single parent with a mortgage, who already struggles to cover the household expenditure – these changes will make things significantly harder. Reversing them could have a positive, material impact on their ability to stay afloat and avoid debts becoming problematic.

Cuts to support for new parents

It is well understood that at the point of having a new child, family incomes get stretched and additional support is needed to see people through this exciting – but very costly – period. In the UK, families with children aged between nought and four are at the highest risk of poverty, with more than a third of children in families with very young children, living below the poverty line.

For some families in our interviews, the additional costs and reduced income associated with having young children was a key driver of problem debt. This is evidenced particularly strongly in 'The Gift' (Chapter Sixteen), where Debbie was quite explicit in linking her family's journey into problem debt with the arrival of her third child, Bobby, and the reduced pay alongside extra outgoings this entailed.

Given this, it is right that in recent years, extra support has been made available in the benefits system for families with new children. This extra support has included things like the Sure Start Maternity Grant (a one-off grant of £500 to help with the costs of a new child), a Health in Pregnancy Grant (of £190) to help expectant mothers to eat healthily during pregnancy, and the baby element of Child Tax Credit (£545), which provided additional support through the tax credits system for the first year of a child's life. The last Labour government had also planned to introduce a 'toddler element' from 2012 (of £209) to provide extra help for children aged between one and two. Such extra support also included the Child Trust Fund, which provided a £500 savings voucher for children in low-income families (with additional payments for children with disabilities). This provided a small nest egg for children in these families, so that when they grew up they would have some savings with which to start their adult life.

However, extra support like this has been severely curtailed more recently. By 2015, the Sure Start Maternity Grant had been restricted to the first child only, and the Health in Pregnancy Grant and the

Child Trust Fund had been abolished. The baby element of Child Tax Credit had also gone, and the plans for a toddler element had been reversed. In total this could amount to cuts in maternity benefits of £1,735 over pregnancy and the first year of a child's life alone. To give families like those in our stories a fighting chance of staying afloat when they expand, these cuts would need to be reversed.

Debts to public authorities

Some of the stories in this book speak to problems surrounding debts to the public sector, either to the national government as a result of issues with benefits such as tax credits, or to local government, often as a result of debts on Council Tax bills. Problems are often linked to the administration of debts.

Taking each of these in turn, many tax credit claimants face 'overpayments' on their awards – debts caused by being paid too much and being asked to pay it back. We saw this in 'Juggling' (Chapter Twelve), where Maryam had been paid tax credits that she was not entitled to on more than one occasion. To reduce the likelihood of overpayments occurring, the tax credit system has a built-in a 'buffer zone', known as the 'income disregard', which means that a household's income can rise by a given amount during a year without affecting their tax credit entitlement. Since 2010, the size of the overpayments buffer zone has been reduced – first from £25,000 to £10,000, then to £5,000, and then to £2,500 (Royston, 2017). Unsurprisingly, as the income disregard has been reduced, tax credit overpayments have increased. In 2014–15, more than one in three claimants were facing an overpayment, and a total of £1.7 billion of overpayments were generated. Fixing problems like these with the administration of tax credits would prevent families from accruing these kinds of debts.

Debts to local government are also evident in some of our stories – in particular in 'Who cares?' (Chapter Five) where we saw care leaver Steven fall into arrears with his Council Tax bill, and in 'The gift' (Chapter Sixteen) where we learned about Debbie and her family's experience of Council Tax debt.

Until recently, support with Council Tax covered the costs of Council Tax in full for those with no income or savings (other than out-of-work benefit income such as Jobseeker's Allowance). From 2013, responsibility for administering the benefit was passed to councils. As a result, each council was asked to produce a local scheme of support (called a Council Tax Reduction scheme). However, the government also decided to simultaneously reduce the money available to local authorities for providing Council Tax Reduction, by 10%.[7] The Local Government Association (2015) has found that this meant that there was a £1 billion shortfall between the money needed to retain the pre-2013 scheme and the money actually available to councils for delivering the new schemes. The impact of this reduction in support has been serious, for claimants and councils. At the same time as Council Tax Benefit was localised and cut, there was a significant rise in Council Tax arrears, and further increases the following year. By 2015, councils faced arrears of £2.7 billion – over 10% more than the total arrears in 2013, just before the localisation of Council Tax Benefit. In this context, it is not surprising that councils pursue aggressive approaches to debt collection. The Children's Society (2015b) reported that in 2012/13 there were a total of 1.9 million court summons for Council Tax debt, but that following the localisation of Council Tax Benefit this increased by a third, to 2.6 million.

For people like Steven and Debbie who have struggled as a specific result of falling into arrears on their Council Tax, support that covered the cost of it in full, and less aggressive means of collecting debts owed, could make a tangible difference.

Breathing space

In most of the stories in this book, families have been unable to manage their debts because they do not (or no longer) have the money to do so. They need decent, stable incomes to be able to afford the cost of living and avoid falling into problem debt.

However, for those who do fall into problem debt, the impact of struggling with a low income can be further exacerbated by additional interest, charges stacking up and pressure applied by creditors. This is why The Children's Society called our five-year campaign on families facing problem debt the Debt Trap. In such cases, better support in dealing with the debts themselves – in addition to addressing problems caused by low income – could make a real difference.

Such support should take the form of a Breathing Space scheme to provide respite from additional interest, fees, charges and collection activities, for families unable to manage their debt repayments. In particular, such a scheme could help families for whom it is the pressure of aggressive collection activities – such as those described in 'The Others' (Chapter Eight), 'The downside of help' (Chapter Thirteen) and 'The gift' (Chapter Sixteen) – and the interest and charges levied against the debts themselves, that are making managing their debts problematic.

On some occasions, families can enter into voluntary arrangements with their creditors to provide some breathing space, but too often such an approach fails – all it takes is aggressive action from one creditor to derail a household's carefully arranged plan to resolve their debts. Aggressive creditor activities force families to cut back on the basics, resort to more or worse credit, and fall further behind on bills, with added stress and anxiety for them and their children.

Legally binding protections do apply for those who go insolvent because it is too unrealistic for them to repay their debts and their situation is unlikely to change in the future. But insolvency is only the right option for a minority of people seeking help with their debts. Most, given appropriate time and space, are not looking to have their debts written off and could be significantly helped via an interim protection scheme that gives them space to recover from relatively short-term changes to personal circumstances and make affordable repayments on their debts.

The Children's Society and StepChange Debt Charity (2014) have proposed that a legally binding scheme should be introduced, with two parts. The first part would offer an initial respite period from interest, charges, collections and enforcement action. This would, first, provide the time for individuals in debt crisis to get advice on the best way to resolve their debts, and second, provide the time for individuals to stabilise their finances and recover from a period of financial difficulty. The second part would provide an extension of these protections, in cases where indebted families had set up a plan to sustainably repay their debts.

At the time of writing, in February 2018, the government had accepted our proposals to set up a Breathing Space scheme. The Children's Society and StepChange Debt Charity are working to ensure that the scheme that is established works as effectively as it possibly can.

While a Breathing Space scheme will not address the fundamental issue of inadequate income, it could go a long way to preventing some families from falling into the debt trap, by alleviating the pressure of debt repayments.

Interest-free credit in a crisis

For many of the families whose stories we have shared in this book, a Breathing Space scheme may not even have been required if they had had access to affordable credit when they really needed it. In these cases, problems are often the result of families having no option than to turn to high-cost credit.

For a number of decades, the state has had a role in providing interest-free credit to families in need of additional help. Such credit, provided through the Discretionary Social Fund, includes credit for families who have been receiving certain out-of-work benefits for at least six months and, as a result, lack the basic income they need to purchase essential items (these are known as Budgeting Loans or Budgeting Advances). In the past, it also included credit for families in need of emergency support (known as Crisis Loans). Access to such interest-free credit helps to ensure that families in need do not have to turn to high-cost borrowing when they can least afford the charges this entails.

However, recent changes have substantially reduced the amount of interest-free credit available for families facing a crisis. In particular,

Crisis Loans were abolished from 2013, with some money made available to local authorities to provide alternative provision.

The complexity of administering a local loans scheme has meant that very few local authorities have introduced credit provision, most preferring, in very restricted circumstances, to provide benefits in kind (such as used furniture or food aid) instead. Some local authorities no longer have any replacement scheme. At the same time, real-term spending on Budgeting Loans has fallen significantly since 2010. Overall lending has reduced from around £790 million in 2009/10, to around £410 million in 2016/17 – a reduction of nearly 50% (End Child Poverty, 2017).

Providing better access to interest-free credit for families on low incomes could play a key role in preventing them from turning to high-cost credit, and thus interrupt the spiral of unaffordable debt repayments.

The work of The Children's Society

Over the past few years, through its Debt Trap campaign, The Children's Society has worked hard to reduce the impacts that problem debt can have on the lives of children and families. In some cases we have been successful: the government has accepted the proposal that The Children's Society and StepChange Debt Charity put forward for a Breathing Space scheme for families experiencing problem debt; over 60 local authorities around the country have exempted care leavers from paying Council Tax until they reach the age of 25; and five of the 'big six' energy companies have made at least one change to debt collection practices, which we recommended in our report *Show some warmth* (The Children's Society, 2015a).[8]

But there is more work to be done: many councils have not yet exempted care leavers from paying Council Tax; energy companies could go even further to support vulnerable families; and our call to ban payday loan adverts from children's television has not yet been taken up by the advertising watchdog, although it has committed to reviewing the content of adverts to see whether some of them promote irresponsible borrowing to vulnerable people. On these and other, related issues, charities like The Children's Society will continue to campaign for change. Our hope is that by sharing the stories in this book, more people will be inspired and equipped to make that change happen.

Notes

[1] A debt is 'secured' if it is backed by an asset, usually a house, and 'unsecured' if there is no asset that can be used as collateral to guarantee repayment if the borrower defaults.

[2] To understand where our sample sits in the broader population of people living with problem debt, see Money Advice Service (2013).

[3] See Royston (2017) for a detailed account of changes to the benefits system.

[4] Inspired by the opening line to Vonnegut's (1969) *Slaughterhouse five*: 'Listen. Billy Pilgrim has come unstuck in time.'

[5] So titled in reference to *The gift* – a book by French social anthropologist Marcel Mauss (1990), in which he explores how the reciprocal exchange of objects between people functions to build and enhance social relationships.

[6] For a more detailed discussion of these, and other, changes to LHA, see Royston (2017).

[7] See Adam et al (2014) for evidence that in some cases the reduction was actually as high as 14%.

[8] For more details on this, visit https://www.childrenssociety.org.uk/what-you-can-do/campaign-for-change/show-some-warmth-fuel-debt-and-families

References

Adam, S., Browne, S., Jeffs, W. and Joyce, R. (2014) *Council Tax support schemes in England: What did local authorities choose, and with what effects?*, London: Institute for Fiscal Studies.

Aitkenhead, D. (2012) 'Abhijit Banerjee: "The poor, probably rightly, see that their chances of getting somewhere different are rather minimal"', *The Guardian*, 22 April.

Ambrose, J. (2017) 'Energy suppliers battered as price cap legislation moves ahead', *The Telegraph*, 4 October, www.telegraph.co.uk/business/2017/10/04/energy-suppliers-battered-price-cap-legislation-moves-ahead/

Aries, P. (1962) *Centuries of childhood: A social history of family life*, London: Jonathan Cape.

Banerjee, A.V. and Duflo, E. (2011) *Poor economics: A radical rethinking of the way to fight global poverty*, New York City, NY: PublicAffairs.

BBC News (2017) *UK inflation at highest since April 2012*, BBC News, 17 October, www.bbc.co.uk/news/business-41649498

Become (2018) 'Being a care leaver', www.becomecharity.org.uk/care-the-facts/being-a-care-leaver/

Belfield, C., Britton, J., Dearden, L. and van der Erve, L. (2017) *Higher education funding in England: Past, present and options for the future*, London: Institute for Fiscal Studies.

Bourdieu, P. (1996) 'Cultural reproduction and social reproduction', in R. Brown (ed) *Knowledge, education and cultural change*, London: Routledge, pp 71–112.

Bourgois, P. (1995) *In search of respect: Selling crack in El Barrio*, Cambridge: Cambridge University Press.

Bradley, A. and Marjoribanks, D. (2017) *In too deep: An investigation into debt and relationships*, Doncaster: Relate.

Buchan, L. (2017) 'Benefits freeze will "drive nearly half a million people into poverty"', *Independent*, 9 October, www.independent. co.uk/news/uk/politics/benefits-freeze-uk-half-a-million-people-poverty-government-lift-welfare-changes-a7990036.html

Byron, T. (2014) *The skeleton cupboard: The making of a clinical psychologist*, London: Macmillan.

Centre for Social Justice (2015) *Finding their feet: Equipping care leavers to reach their potential*, London: Centre for Social Justice.

Citizens Advice (2017) *Stuck in debt: Why do people get trapped in problem debt?*, London: Citizens Advice.

CMA (Competition & Markets Authority) (2015) *Payday lending market investigation*, London: CMA.

CMA (2016) *Energy market investigation: Final report*, London: CMA.

Consumer Financial Protection Bureau (2016) *Financial coaching: A strategy to improve financial well-being*, Washington, DC: Consumer Financial Protection Bureau.

Cunningham, H. (2006) *The invention of childhood*, London: BBC Books.

Davies, S., Finney, A. and Hartfree, Y. (2016) *Paying to be poor: Uncovering the scale and nature of the poverty premium*, Bristol: University of Bristol.

de Santos, R. (2014) *Life on the edge: Towards more resilient family finances*, London: StepChange Debt Charity.

Department for Business, Energy and Industrial Strategy (2017) *Draft Domestic Gas and Electricity (Tariff Cap) Bill*, London: Department for Business, Energy and Industrial Strategy.

Department for Communities and Local Government, Homelessness Statistics, table 773. https://www.gov.uk/government/statistical-data-sets/live-tables-on-homelessness

Department for Communities and Local Government, Homelessness Statistics, table 775. https://www.gov.uk/government/statistical-data-sets/live-tables-on-homelessness

Department for Education (2017) *Children looked after in England including adoption: 2016-2017*, SFR50/2017, London: GOV.UK, https://www.gov.uk/government/statistics/children-looked-after-in-england-including-adoption-2016-to-2017

DWP (Department for Work and Pensions) (2014) *Monitoring the impact of recent measures affecting Housing Benefit and Local Housing Allowances in the private rented sector: The response of landlords*, London: DWP.

Dyson, J. (2010) 'Friendship in practice: girls' work in the Indian Himalayas', *American Ethnologist*, 37(3): 482–98.

End Child Poverty (2017) *Furnishing your home with rent to own*, London: End Child Poverty

Department for Work and Pensions (2017) *Family resources survey 2015/16*, FRS 2015–16. https://www.gov.uk/government/statistics/family-resources-survey-financial-year-201516

FCA (Financial Conduct Authority) (2016) *Credit Card Market Study: Final findings report*, London: FCA.

FCA (2017) 'FCA proposes new rules for credit card firms to help millions of customers get out of persistent debt', press release, 3 April, https://www.fca.org.uk/news/press-releases/fca-proposes-new-rules-help-customers-persistent-debt-credit-cards

Gathergood, J. (2012) 'Debt and depression: causal links and social norm effects', *The Economic Journal*, 122: 1094–114.

Gedikli, C., Bryan, M., Connolly, S., Daniels, K., Watson, D., Semkina, A. and Vaughn, O. (2017) 'Worklessness and wellbeing: what is the evidence?', presented at the Work, Learning and Wellbeing Conference, University of East Anglia, 12 January.

Giddens, A. (1984) *The constitution of society: Outline of the theory of structuration*, Berkeley, CA: University of California Press.

Graeber, D. (2011) *Debt: The first 5,000 years*, New York, NY: Melville House.

Grosz, S. (2014) *The examined life: How we lose and find ourselves*, London: Vintage.

Hartfree, Y. and Collard, S. (2014) *Poverty, debt and credit: An expert-led review*, Bristol: Personal Finance Research Centre, University of Bristol.

Hobbs, G. and Vignoles, A. (2007) *Is free school meal status a valid proxy for socio-economic status (in schools research)?*, London: London School of Economics, Centre for the Economics of Education.

Hood, A. and Waters, T. (2017) *Living standards, poverty and inequality in the UK: 2016-2017 to 2021-2022*, London: Institute for Fiscal Studies.

Jeffrey, C. (2011) 'Geographies of children and youth ii: global youth agency', *Progress in Human Geography*, 36(2): 245–53.

Jensen, T. (2014) 'Welfare commonsense, poverty porn and doxosophy', *Sociological Research Online*, 19(3): 3.

JRF (Joseph Rowntree Foundation) (2015) *UK poverty: Causes, costs and solutions*, York: JRF.

Lane, J. (2016) *A debt effect? How is unmanageable debt related to other problems in people's lives?*, London: Citizens Advice.

Lewis, M., Keefe, J. and Curphey, M. (2017) *Mental health & debt 2017*, London: MoneySavingExpert.com, https://images6. moneysavingexpert.com/images/documents/mentalhealthguide_ new_may_2017.pdf?_ga=2.120351688.1728910436.1516027494- 309666249.1508790367

Lister, R. (2013) 'How the language of welfare poisoned our social security', Compass, 2 April, https://www.compassonline.org.uk/ how-the-language-of-welfare-poisoned-our-social-security/

Local Government Association (2015) *Council Tax support: The story continues*, London: Local Government Association.

Loopstra, R. and Lalor, D. (2017) *Financial insecurity, food insecurity, and disability: The profile of people receiving emergency food assistance from The Trussell Trust Foodbank Network in Britain*, London: Trussell Trust.

Mahony, S. (2018) *Searching for a better life: Growing up in the slums of Bangkok*, New York, NY: Berghahn Books.

Main, G. and Pople, L. (2011) *Missing out: A child centred analysis of material deprivation and subjective well-being*, London: The Children's Society.

Mason, R. (2015) 'Cameron vows not to slash child benefit after earlier failures to rule out cut', *The Guardian*, 1 May, www.theguardian.com/society/2015/may/01/david-cameron-child-benefit-no-cuts-vow-general-election

Mauss, M. (1990) *The gift: Forms and functions of exchange in archaic societies*, London: Routledge.

Mental Health Foundation (2018) 'Debt and mental health', https://www.mentalhealth.org.uk/a-to-z/d/debt-and-mental-health

Money Advice Service (2013) *Personalising the debt sector: A segmentation of the over-indebted population*, London: Money Advice Service.

Montgomery, H. (2009) *An Introduction to childhood: Anthropological perspectives on children's lives*, Chichester: Wiley-Blackwell.

NAO (National Audit Office) (2015) *Care leavers' transition to adulthood: Report by the Comptroller and Auditor General*, London: NAO.

NAO (2016) *Local welfare provision*, London: NAO.

Ofgem (2014) *State of the market assessment*, London: Ofgem.

O'Leary, J. (2017) 'How have wages changed over the past decade?', Full Fact, 19 October, https://fullfact.org/economy/how-have-wages-changed/

Patrick, R. (2017) *For whose benefit? The everyday realities of welfare reform*, Bristol: Policy Press.

Rayner, G., Morley, K. and Ambrose, J. (2017) '"Unfair" energy companies raise prices by 37pc before Theresa May can bring in price cap', *The Telegraph*, 8 May, www.telegraph.co.uk/news/2017/05/08/unfair-energy-companies-raise-prices-37pc-theresa-may-can-bring/

Rees, G. and Main, G. (eds) (2015) *Children's views on their lives and well-being in 15 countries: An initial report on the Children's Worlds survey, 2013-14*, York: Children's Worlds Project (ISCWeB).

Relate (2017) In too deep: An investigation into debt and relationships, London: Relate.

Rethink Mental Illness (2017) 'Debt and money management', https://www.rethink.org/living-with-mental-illness/money-issues-benefits-employment/debt-and-money-management

Royal College of Psychiatrists (2017) 'Debt and mental health', www.rcpsych.ac.uk/healthadvice/problemsdisorders/debtandmentalhealth.aspx

Royston, S. (2017) *Broken benefits: What's gone wrong with welfare reform?*, Bristol: Policy Press.

Scott, J. (1985) *Weapons of the weak: Everyday forms of peasant resistance*, New Haven, CT: Yale University Press.

Scott Paul, A. (2016) 'Talking about poverty – time to rethink our approach?', blog, 14 April, Joseph Rowntree Foundation, https://www.jrf.org.uk/blog/talking-about-poverty-time-rethink-our-approach

Spencer, N., Nieboer, J. and Elliott, A. (2015) *Wired for imprudence: Behavioural hurdles to financial capability and challenges for financial education*, London: RSA Action and Research Centre.

StepChange Debt Charity (2015) *An action plan on problem debt: How the next UK government can reduce the £8.3 billion social cost of problem debt*, London: StepChange Debt Charity.

StepChange Debt Charity (2017) *Statistics mid-year book: Personal debt Jan-June 2017*, London: StepChange Debt Charity.

Surtees, J. (2015) *Becoming a nation of savers: Keeping families out of debt by helping them prepare for a rainy day*, London: StepChange Debt Charity.

The Children's Society (2014) *Playday not payday: Protecting children from irresponsible payday loan advertising*, London: The Children's Society.

The Children's Society (2015a) *Show some warmth: Exposing the damaging impact of energy debt on children*, London: The Children's Society.

The Children's Society (2015b) *The wolf at the door: How Council Tax debt collection is harming children*, London: The Children's Society.

The Children's Society (2016a) *The damage of debt: The impact of money worries on children's mental health and wellbeing*, London: The Children's Society.

The Children's Society (2016b) *The future of family incomes: How key tax and welfare changes will affect families to 2020*, London: The Children's Society.

The Children's Society (2016c) *The good childhood report*, London: The Children's Society.

The Children's Society and National Energy Action (2015) *Making a house a home: Providing affordable warmth solutions for children and families living in fuel poverty*, Solihull: Affordable Warmth Solutions.

The Children's Society and StepChange Debt Charity (2014) *The debt trap: Exposing the impact of problem debt on children*, London: The Children's Society.

Titheridge, H., Christie, N., Mackett, R., Oviedo Hernández, D. and Ye, R. (2014) *Transport and poverty: A review of the evidence*, London: UCL.

Townsend, P. (1979) *Poverty in the United Kingdom*, London: Allen Lane and Penguin Books.

UNICEF (2005) 'Childhood defined', UNICEF, https://www.unicef.org/sowc05/english/childhooddefined.html

Vaughan, A. (2017) 'May's pledge on "rip off" energy prices keeps UK in dark over cap on bills, The Guardian, 4 October, https://www.theguardian.com/money/2017/oct/04/theresa-may-pledge-rip-off-energy-prices-uk-cap

Vonnegut, K. (1969) *Slaughterhouse five*, New York, NY: Dell Publishing.

Wacquant, L. (2002) 'Review symposium: scrutinizing the street: poverty, morality, and the pitfalls of urban ethnography', *American Journal of Sociology*, 107(6): 1468–32.

Willis, P. (1977) *Learning to labour: How working class kids get working class jobs*, New York, NY: Columbia University Press.

Yeats, WB, 1899, 'Cloths of heaven', in *The wind among the reeds*, London: Elkin Mathews.

Index